THE

PASTOR IN THE SICK-ROOM.

THREE LECTURES

DELIVERED AT PRINCETON THEOLOGICAL SEMINARY, MARCH, 1892.

BY

JOHN D. WELLS, D.D.,

SENIOR PASTOR OF SOUTH THIRD STREET PRESBYTERIAN CHURCH, BROOKLYN, N. Y.

Solid Ground Christian Books
Birmingham, Alabama

SOLID GROUND CHRISTIAN BOOKS
PO Box 660132, Vestavia Hills, AL 35266
205-443-0311
sgcb@charter.net
http://solid-ground-books.com

The Pastor in the Sick-Room:
Ministering the Gospel on the Brink of Eternity

by John D. Wells (1815-1903)

Taken from the 1893 edition by the Presbyterian Board of Publication and Sabbath-School Work, Philadelphia, PA

COVER IMAGE: The sick bed of Adolphe Monod, gifted French Reformed preacher who spent the final nine months of his life in a sick bed, and from which he spoke each Lord's Day afternoon to those of his congregation who gathereed before him each week.

Published by Solid Ground Christian Books

Classic Reprints Series

First printing of new edition September 2004

ISBN: 1-932474-49-8

Manufactured in the United States of America

PREFACE.

THIS little volume is made up of three lectures delivered to the students of Princeton Theological Seminary in March, 1892. They are now published at the request of the professors who heard them.

Fully recognizing their defects, I offer them as a contribution to a very important branch of pastoral service, hoping that other pastors of large experience may supplement them for the benefit of younger brethren, the salvation of souls and the glory of God.

J. D. W.

PARSONAGE, BROOKLYN, N. Y.,
1892.

CONTENTS.

LECTURE I.

THE DIFFERENCE BETWEEN THE SICK-BED AND THE DEATH-BED.

LECTURE II.

SALVATION POSSIBLE, AND IN MANY CASES PROBABLE, ON THE DEATH-BED.

LECTURE III.

WRONG TREATMENT OF THE SICK AND DYING; RIGHT TREATMENT OF THE SAME; USES THAT MAY BE MADE OF THEIR EXPERIENCE.

LECTURE I.

The Difference between the Sick-Bed and the Death-Bed.

THE PASTOR IN THE SICK-ROOM.

LECTURE I.

INTRODUCTORY.

I COME to you, brethren, simply as a pastor. I hope to give you three lectures, not with the learning of books or of the schools—although these are invaluable sources of information on many subjects—but out of many years' experience with the sick and the dying. I ask you to interrupt me at any point in my reading of the lectures if you think it important to do so, or to question me at the close of each lecture, should it occur to you that anything of which I may speak requires clearer, fuller or different statement.

Long before my ordination and installation I was drawn into the presence of the sick and the dying. The first encouragement I remember to have had in laboring for the salvation of one on a death-bed was in this place, while a student in this theological seminary. Hearing that a young mulatto barber was sick and that no one called on him, I ventured to do so. I saw at a glance that there were unmistakable symptoms of pulmonary disease, and I determined to be frank and faithful in dealing with his soul.

He was lying on his bed in full dress, with a guitar at his side and secular music within easy reach. I noticed, too, that on the fingers of one hand there was a profusion of rings. After a few words of ordinary conversation I asked if he had a physician. Learning that he was under the care of a competent man, I asked further if he had been told what was the nature of his sickness. He answered, no, but that he would like to be informed. I then felt free to ask if he wished my opinion, and being assured that he did, I told him tenderly but plainly that I feared his disease was incurable, and that I would very much like to know if he was prepared for the life following this, which was evidently very frail and uncertain. He replied that he had given the matter no serious thought, and was wholly unprepared for leaving the world.

Then, as fully and as earnestly as possible, I instructed him out of the Scriptures on the deceitfulness and desperate wickedness of the heart; the just exposure of the unpardoned sinner to the penalty of God's law; the necessity of the birth from above; the willingness and ability of Jesus Christ to save to the uttermost all who come unto God by him; and the presence and power of the Holy Spirit to make the sinner a new creature in Christ Jesus. I told him that he must take the Saviour at his word, repent of his sins and believe the good news of salvation without money and without price, coming to Jesus Christ on his own invitation: "Come unto me, all ye that labor and are heavy laden, and I will give you rest."

After prayer, and as I was leaving, I begged him to cast himself as he was upon the mercy of God in Jesus Christ; to do it without delay, and to have no doubts; to confess his sinfulness and transgressions, and to plead for the salvation that would certainly come to him with the knowledge and belief that the blood of Jesus Christ the Son of God cleanseth us from all sin.

Being very anxious for him, I called the next day, but before I could pass from the door of his room to the bed where he lay he reached out his hand and greeted me with words of cheerful hope. He assured me that he had found peace in believing. I feared that he was mistaken—that he had received the Word with joy, but had no depth of conviction or true sorrow for sin or faith in the Saviour. Therefore I carefully questioned him regarding his views of sin, of repentance, of the new birth, and of the person, the offices and the sufferings of Christ as the only Saviour of sinners. As the result, I could only believe, with wonder and gratitude, that he had indeed so quickly passed from death unto life. There was a change even in the aspect of his room and person. Old things had passed away; behold! all things had become new. The guitar and music and rings had disappeared, though I had not said a word about them. Other persons of larger experience than myself were taken to see and converse with him. All were constrained to believe that the change was real and saving. The effect on the condition of his health was remarkable. He rose from his bed, lived through the spring and summer, and late in the fall it pleased the Saviour to call him home.

The day before his departure, I said to him, "James, you are near the grave; does it seem dark and forbidding to you?" He answered pleasantly, "I am looking beyond the grave, and there I see nothing but light; I am not afraid of death and the grave."

His death was very peaceful. There was no cloud upon his reason and no darkness in his soul. With an unshaken trust in the Lord Jesus Christ he entered the river, and found the everlasting arms about him all the way over.*

My close connection with the case of this humble barber has had its influence upon my treatment of the sick and dying during all these later years. With hundreds I have gone as far as possible in their drawing near to the grave. From the bed-sides of many who were sick not unto death I have come back a sad witness, as their after-life unmistakably proved, that their good resolutions were as the morning cloud and the early dew. An interest ofttimes growing to fascination has kept me near the sufferers rather to help than to see and hear. Some of the rarest scenes this side of heaven are in the rooms of sickness and death. Others are too appalling to admit of description.

The results of observation and reflection in many and varying circumstances can hardly fail to be useful to the living, and especially to those who expect to minister in the pulpit and the private house. Some of these results, verified by confer-

* See tract, *James the Barber*, No. 673, published by the American Tract Society many years ago.

ence with other pastors, I have recorded, and hope to make known to you. Cases of exceptional interest have compelled me to change my views regarding the possibility, and even probability, of salvation coming, by God's blessing, to those who are sick and soon to die, when they who watch for their souls are wise and faithful. For this reason I ask a hearing from you, dear brethren, who are preparing for the sacred office of the Christian ministry and the responsible work of pastors. I am to speak especially, though not exclusively, of those who are believed to be without Christ when they fall sick or are fatally hurt. At best their condition is desolate in the extreme. Some are suddenly bereft of reason; others are stupefied by narcotics or excited by fever or stimulants. The Adversary may assail them with all his subtlety, malignity and might because he sees that he has but a short time. Possibly they may be cut off from all communication with those who would gladly point and lead them to Christ. By these and, it may be, other difficulties they are beset. Left to themselves, they are in danger of becoming victims of fatal delusions. If they have many teachers and conflicting counsels, they can hardly fail to be confused and distracted. They may not have a single competent and faithful guide, and, failing to lay hold on eternal life, at last die in their sins.

But I firmly and gladly believe that many sinners are called and justified and saved on beds of death. In the fond hope that the number may be largely increased by God's blessing on wise and earnest efforts of Christian ministers and others, I ask to be heard here, where, fifty years ago, I sat with many others at the feet of Dr. Archibald Alexander, Dr. Samuel Miller, Dr. Charles Hodge and Dr. Joseph Addison Alexander, all of blessed memory.

The main subject of this lecture is *The Sick-Bed* and *The Death-Bed,* with the *difference* between *them in relation to salvation.*

Whatever may be the nature of sickness, the hand of God is in it. Second causes, with which we and others have so much to do, are not beyond the control of the Great First Cause. Malarial and all other diseases, with calamities of every kind, are subject to the divine will. And the living, exalted Christ is given to be Head over all things to the Church. This great truth ought to be recognized and prized more than it is. What can be more comforting when sickness or peril comes to ourselves? So, too, it is our encouragement in efforts for the salvation of others who are or seem to be not far from death. Yet truth requires me to say that a sick-bed is a most unfavorable place for laying hold on eternal life.

To the proof of this I ask your earnest attention.

1. The invitations and promises of the Bible are addressed mainly to persons supposed to be in health.

The young are expected to remember their Creator in the days of their youth, while the evil days come not, nor the years draw nigh when they shall severally say, "I have no pleasure in them." These "evil days" come sooner or later, with bodily weakness and mental distress. If greatly delayed, they come at last, in many if not most cases, with the decay and depression of old age. It is a fact abundantly verified that few turn to the Lord and find the strong consolations of good hope after the high meridian of life. "I love them that love me, and those that seek me early shall find me." This sweet assurance of personal Wisdom is in perfect keeping with what Jesus said long after, taking little children to his arms: "Suffer the little children to come unto me, and forbid them not, for of such is the kingdom of God."

2. The revealed plan for saving the lost sup-

poses them, for the most part, gathered in places where the word of salvation is publicly heralded. So it was on the day of Pentecost, when three thousand were added to the Church; and a little after, when other thousands swelled the number of disciples.

God's true ministers are ambassadors for Christ. They are messengers, heralds, authorized and commanded to make known the terms of peace, to publish the glad tidings of great joy. Of course they are required to preach the gospel from house to house as well as in public places; to single individuals, young and old, as they have opportunity. Yet their great commission supposes them to have access to the multitudes where they are gathered together, and not chiefly in rooms darkened by sickness. It is true that large numbers of the unsaved gather on funeral occasions in private houses or places of public worship, out of respect for their fellows whose bodies are about to be buried, or from sympathy with the afflicted, or from a morbid curiosity, and on these occasions the gospel may be faithfully and earnestly preached. But I believe that saving benefits rarely follow. A pastor of great devotion and large experience has left his testimony that he never knew a sinner to be awakened and brought to Christ as the result of attendance upon a funeral service. His explanation is this: While it is ever true that God waits to be gracious and has no pleasure in the death of the wicked, it is also true that he will not suffer himself to be dishonored, and the gospel of his grace neglected, by those who will not meet him in his house on ordinary occasions, but who are not willing to absent themselves from services for the burial of the dead, for reasons already given.

It has been my aim throughout my ministry to make funeral services helpful to the living for the consolation of the bereaved and the salvation of the lost. In a single case, conducting the service for the burial of a merchant who had taken his own life, I had reason to hope that one of his salesmen was savingly impressed by the words spoken and the awful solemnity of the occasion. He was received into the communion of our church on confession of Christ, but after some years of consistent living in connection with us he disappeared, and we know not where he is, if he is still among the living.*

*Since delivering this lecture I have heard of an eminent pastor, whose name I do not feel at liberty to give, who thinks that under his ministry many have been won to Christ by the gospel preached on funeral occasions.

3. Persons to whom the gospel comes with saving power are supposed to be in circumstances favorable to active and grateful service to their new Master.

Thus, standing idle in the market-place at any hour, they are called to work in the vineyard of the Lord and receive the wages that he never fails to give to those who serve him.

Entrusted with talents one or many, they are to use them for increase, that they may give account with joy, and not with grief, and have rule over cities according to their several ability.

Engaged in the lawful work of their farms or merchandise, or even satisfied with social delights in their families, they are called to a feast, "a great supper," by One who puts no hindrance in the way of honorable pursuits and domestic happiness, but by his gracious feasts of love prepares his guests for active service and large rewards.

In this and other parables of our Lord there is no suggestion of sickness and the interruption of the work of life.

4. It is an historical fact that the family of God on earth has its chief increase from those who are strong and in health. Under the ministry of Christ and those who served him in the early years of this

ministration of the Spirit, there were many instances of individuals, whose names are preserved in the Gospels and the Acts of the Apostles, turning to the Lord. But they were not persons subdued to sobriety and unworldliness by sickness, possibly with death in near prospect. The miracles of healing wrought by Jesus were largely meant to show that the Son of Man had power on earth to forgive sins and to prepare witnesses who would show forth the praises of him who had not merely healed their sickness, but called them from death unto life.

When the Holy Ghost was given to the eleven and their associates, godly men and women, a way was soon made for them to the people of Samaria and Cæsarea, of Antioch and the cities of Asia, of Macedonia and Achaia and other parts of Europe.

To this day, as the so-called "sacramental host," under the commission and command of our Lord, we are required to put on the panoply of God, to fight our enemies, which are also his, and to go forth, taking possession of villages, cities, continents, the world, in the name of our Master.

In a large view, it seems almost as if the God of salvation lost sight of the sick-bed in seeking children for his household on the earth.

5. In further proof that the bed of sickness and

death is not a favorable place for finding the salvation of God, we should keep in mind the nature of the gospel.

It is the good news of salvation by faith in Jesus Christ. But it is also a collection of precious truths to be learned, believed and lived. They relate to the being, the character and the perfections of God; to the spirituality of his law; to the person, offices and redemptive work of God's dear Son, our Lord Jesus Christ; to the person and work of the Holy Spirit, to whom it belongs to convict us of sin, to quicken us together with Christ and to persuade and enable us to embrace him as he is offered to us in the gospel.

Here, therefore, is a call for sinful man to hear, learn, believe and practice the truth. Happily, his doing this does not depend on the strength of his intellect. I knew a young man, hardly half-witted, whose whole nature seemed to be demoralized, if not demonized, who was brought to the Saviour's feet and service under the ministry of young Mr. Malcom, a student of this seminary while I was here, and made eminently helpful in a great revival that resulted in the salvation of many souls.

Still, it remains obviously true that persons

weakened, confused and sometimes demented by diseases of the body or tortured by severe pains are not in a favorable condition to receive instruction, or even to listen to the most winsome invitations that can be breathed into their ears.

6. A word should be added here about the connection of the body and the mind. They constitute one person. Death parts them, but only for a season. Whatever the change, they will be reunited in the resurrection at the last day. Until death they are held together by a tie never laid bare by the surgeon's scalpel. Loosen the "silver cord" and the body returns to the earth as it was, and the spirit returns unto God who gave it. Still, personality is not destroyed, although it is not what it will be when the body is raised and suited to its new conditions—in light or darkness, with Christ where he is, or severed from him by choice and by his righteous judgment.

How profound, therefore, the mystery of the union of body and spirit during this mortal life! "A sound mind in a sound body" has grown into a proverb. Its truth should arrest and hold the attention of every one who watches for souls, and of all who are yet to find the eternal life in Jesus Christ or die in their sins.

There are some sicknesses and hurts by which the nerves of sensation are so tortured that the sufferer cries out in his agony and cannot order his thoughts as he would. The tenderest ministry of kindred and pastor utterly fails to find in such a time a convenient season for urging or giving heed to the claims of the Saviour. The patient Job exclaimed, "He breaketh me with breach upon breach; he runneth upon me like a giant."

There are depressing diseases by which the powers of life are weakened almost to extinction. The blood flows with feeble current through arteries and veins. It may be vitiated by unhealthful secretions from within or by poisons from without. The lips lose their color and the eyes their lustre. The incubus of unnatural sleep falls upon the patient, and his soul dwells in darkness. He forgets to eat his daily bread. You try in vain to rouse him by the good news of salvation or by any other tidings, and in this condition his body may sleep its last sleep.

Supposing him to live, it is well if the shadow of an oppressive melancholy does not fall upon him. In his brightest moments the hope of any change for the better may die in his heart. I have known Christians of large experience, in these trying circumstances, compelled to say that if their salvation depended upon the putting forth of any effort to receive the gospel, they must perish. They could only await the issue of their sickness without fear, knowing whom they had believed, and persuaded that he was able to keep that which they had committed unto him against the day of their departure and the time of his second coming. Indeed, I have been in this condition myself.

Some diseases excite and exhilarate. Pulmonary affections and many fevers are apt to do this. The circulation is quickened. The brain and the whole nervous system are roused to unwonted activity. The mind may be surcharged with thoughts that do not obey the laws of reason. The wildest delirium often follows, and the patient lives for the time in a world to which the most intimate friends can gain no access. It is painful to witness the wanderings of the mind even when you have reason to believe that the life is hid with Christ in God, for sometimes they seem to indicate a character the very opposite of that which you supposed belonged to the sufferer. It is more than painful—even appalling—to know that in these circumstances persons who have shown no signs of an interest in the Saviour apparently become his loving disciples, and yet with returning health retain no recollection of their thoughts, emotions or words. Many instances have been related to me, by pastors and physicians, of persons in sickness passing through all the stages of awakening, conviction, conversion and the joyful confession of Christ as their Saviour, and yet, on recovering, they have been unable to recall the facts of the most recent past, and have proved by their manner of living afterward that no saving change had been wrought in them.

In one case, related by the Rev. Benjamin Holt Rice, D. D., then pastor of the Presbyterian church in Princeton, a young lady, the belle of the place (not Princeton), a gay and worldly person, was stricken with typhoid fever. Dr. Rice was a young pastor then, and, having been called to visit her, did so from day to day. At last it was thought she must die. Believing herself that the end was near, she called to her bedside the members of her family, who knew the vain life she had lived. She told them that she had found peace in believing; that she believed her sins were forgiven for Jesus' sake, and that she was about to depart to be for ever with him. Bidding them all good-bye, she begged them to meet her in heaven, and then quietly waited for the change.

Her pastor had no doubt that she was a sinner saved by grace. He parted with her in the glad hope of finding her at last and for ever among the redeemed in heaven. Calling the day after, supposing that she had passed away, he found, to his surprise, that the crisis of her disease had passed and that she was convalescent. He thought it wise, therefore, to discontinue his daily visits for a while. When at last he called and made reference to the change in her views and feelings, he was appalled to hear from her own lips that she had not the slightest recollection of his visits or of anything she had said leading him and her family to hope that she was a child of God. She returned to her old ways of living, and not until many years had passed did she earnestly seek and, as she hoped, find the Saviour.

On relating the particulars of this case to an aged Christian physician, he matched it by a similar case, hardly less striking, and reminded me that in the delirium of fever men and women of whose piety there is no reason to have any doubt give utterance to words not at all in keeping with their real character.

7. I may not pass without notice in this connection a fact which every pastor knows to his sorrow

—that some persons falling sick, and very anxious to recover, are unwilling to have a word spoken to them on the subject of religion, or prayer offered in their presence, because in such services there is a suggestion that they may not recover. They do not consider that a pastor who is wise and faithful knows much of the sick-room, and comes to them, if not hindered, only for their help. And they may have yet to learn that a good hope of eternal life is a wonderful remedial agent for the suffering body. I am sorry to add that some physicians do not seem to know this, and would even exclude pastors from the rooms of their patients if they could.

So we have this anomaly—it is worse: I believe it is a wile of the devil—men wait for sickness, proposing then to give earnest heed to the truth of God's word and the salvation of their souls. Then, when sickness comes, they shrink from hearing the message of salvation or the prayer of faith, lest they should be compelled to think that they may die and that they are not prepared for the great change. So they rob themselves of all opportunities of salvation. If they recover, they are in danger of being hardened in impenitence and unbelief. Dying, they go unprepared into the presence of God.

8. It belongs to this part of our subject to make brief reference to the well-known effects of medicines on persons who are sick.

The effects vary from the extreme of insensibility and unconsciousness to that of intense activity of body and vagaries of mind.

Narcotics produce effects of the one kind, and stimulants those of the other. In the use of either—and both may be indispensable in opposite conditions of the body—the sick are unfitted for serious and continuous thought on the great subject of their salvation and the divinely-appointed means by which they are to secure it. Indeed, they are disqualified for all the ordinary affairs of the present life. If persons have lived without Christ until smitten with their last sickness, and are then stupefied with narcotics or excited by stimulants, they cannot be instructed out of the Scriptures while in either of these two conditions of body and mind. The effort, however, should be made at times of greatest promise, and much prayer should be offered in their behalf. The result may not be known till the great day reveals it. It is wrong to relax effort while life lasts.

9. I conclude this part of my lecture with the statement of a fact verified by numerous pastors—

to wit, that of those who profess to have found Christ on a sick-bed, and afterward recover, not one in a hundred—hardly more than one in a thousand—*consents to be numbered among the confessors of Christ.* I do not include in this sad estimate the many who are alarmed by the seeming approach of death, and express their sorrow for misspent years, making solemn promise of amendment in case they recover. A promise of this kind is an easy expedient for calming a troubled conscience. A deceived and deceitful heart can hardly do worse. In effect it is the present rejection of the living Christ who waits to be gracious. One cannot be too earnest and persistent in telling those who propose to do hereafter what they are not willing to do at once that "Now is the accepted time; behold, now is the day of salvation."

In the intervals of pain caused by acute disease and the depression or excitement consequent upon the use of remedies of different kinds, the words of the glorified Christ, spoken in the demonstration of the Spirit and of power by a loving pastor or friend, may reach the heart: "Behold, I stand at the door and knock; if any man hear my voice and open the door, I will come in to him, and will sup with him and he with me."

The distinction between the sick-bed and the death-bed is easily recognized. In one case the patient recovers and returns to the scenes of his former life; in the other he passes away, and the places that once knew him know him no more for ever.

It is true that diseases and medicines may have precisely the same effect in the two cases. Mortal sickness is often attended by weakness and illusions of the mind quite as serious as any connected with diseases from which persons recover. So, too, the instructions, invitations and promises of Scripture may be as unintelligible to persons sick unto death as to those who continue in life.

From these and other facts and considerations a very sad and often unwarrantable conclusion is drawn—to wit, that because those who profess conversion on beds of sickness and recover are in most cases mistaken in their hopes and professions, therefore those who make the like profession and die find themselves without God and without hope in the other world. This is not a warrantable conclusion. It utterly fails to recognize the difference in the two cases. And because it seems to be the conclusion of great and good men I am the more anxious to mark the difference which is so often overlooked.

1. The difference relates to the two classes of persons.

Those who recover from their sickness have the opportunity of correcting mistakes and verifying results. If they have professed conversion, and, on recovering health, find their hearts still turned away from God, they have strong motives for asking that they may be turned toward him by his saving grace.

If they have made promises of reformation in case of recovery, and are disinclined or unable to break off their sins by righteousness, and therefore continue in their old-time unbelief and transgressions, they have a most impressive lesson on the deceitfulness and desperate wickedness of their hearts, and yet are mercifully spared to profit by the lesson. In many instances they do at last seek and find the salvation of God, as did the young lady of whom Dr. Rice told me.

But no such opportunity remains to those who die. If they are deceived, their day of salvation, we believe, is closed. Certainly no day of deliverance in the near or distant future is revealed. Even those who teach probation after death, and hate the doctrine of any judgment that decides and so fixes human destiny at death, are not understood to open a door of hope to those who die in Christendom, whatever they may do for those who have never read or heard the gospel of the grace of God in this life.

2. The difference is hardly less patent and impressive in relation to the friends of the two classes. It is a painful surprise to a pastor or to any one who has heard the words of the sick telling of peace and hope and heaven, and calling upon kindred to meet them in the presence of Christ, to be told by the persons themselves, a few days later, that they have no recollection of anything that occurred, or of words spoken by them or to them, and to find that in character and life they are what they were before the sickness.

Or if they have only promised reformation if God would spare them, the surprise is hardly less painful to know that their pledge has no binding force with them—that their words spoken to friends and in the ear of God have no power against old habits of evil.

Very different is the case of those who, having professed repentance, faith and hope, or with apparent solemnity and sincerity promised a new life in the service of Christ and their fellows, die, their spirits returning unto God who gave them.

A young lady of exceptional intelligence, a teacher of high grade, with whom I had held very interesting conversations about the salvation of her soul, when near death drew her mother's ear close to her trembling lips, and said in a whisper, "If I recover, I wish to unite with —— Church" (naming one that was not the church, or even the denomination, of her family). That wish —never gratified, for she soon died—was an unspeakable consolation to her Christian parents and to all who knew and loved her. We can neither verify nor disprove the change in her that her words implied until we go ourselves into the other world; and possibly not even then.

But while it comforts us greatly to think that her words to her mother revealed a change which, up to that time, had not been known, we take no hurt ourselves and do no harm to her. Nor do we think her case exceptional. Many children of Christian parents, and others who have had the care of the Church, come to the consciousness of need and the hope of salvation on beds of death.

3. The difference between the two classes of persons so often referred to, as they are related to God, is too great for us to understand. We may reverently think and speak of it.

That some should live and others die depends upon the will of God. Life and death are not accidents. Our times are in his hands, the number of our months is with him. If life is threatened and not taken, God spares it. If it is cut off by disease or calamity, we are taught to say, "Thou turnest man to destruction, and sayest, Return, ye children of men." Is it not like God to spare the guilty who are self-deceived; to let them live that they may come to the knowledge of themselves and lay hold of eternal life; at least to give them further opportunity to know, every one, the plague of his own heart, and the healing of the plague by the grace and blood, the word and Spirit, of the living Christ? And is it not in perfect keeping with what we know by revelation of the love of God that he should desire to have his dear children with him, and that he should call them hence when he knows it is safe to do so? The questions are his own: "Have I any pleasure at all that the wicked should die? saith the Lord God, and not that he should return from his ways and live?" We take him at his word. Not more surely have we hope for the penitent robber, who went from the cross to paradise in reliance on the sure word of Jesus, than for many who go from the bed of death beyond our sight, mourning for their sin, freely making confession and rejoicing that they have found the Saviour, and eternal life in him, though in their last hours.

In any case the difference of which I speak is so great that those who minister to the sick, not knowing whether they are to recover or not, have no right to be indifferent or hopeless because they may have seen many recover and make void all their professions and promises.

At best the sick-bed is not favorable to thought and feeling and decision in relation to the things of God and the eternal life which is his gift in Jesus Christ. But it often proves to be the only place remaining to the sick, and we should act intelligently, prayerfully, persistently and hopefully on the supposition that it is.

As an incentive to the wise and faithful treatment of the sick and dying, of which I hope to speak particularly in the last lecture, I give here some of the contrasted experiences of the wicked and the righteous. In both cases there are great varieties.

Some who die in their sins verify the words of Scripture: "Terrors take hold on him as waters, a tempest stealeth him away in the night. The east wind carrieth him away, and he departeth: and as a storm hurleth him out of his place. For God shall cast upon him and not spare; he would fain flee out of his hand;" "This is the portion of a wicked man with God;" "The wicked is driven away in his wickedness;" "If ye believe not that I am he, said Jesus, ye shall die in your sins."

So I have seen an ungodly man come to his death. He had lived without God in the world. A lovely daughter, dying in the faith of Christ in my presence, called him to her side and secured from him the promise that he would attend the Sunday services of the church where she had found peace in believing. For two or three Sundays he did so, and then relapsed into his old ways. Suddenly, after two or three years of persistent violation of his promise, he was summoned to his death. I was sent for in great haste, and found him in sore pain of body and agony of mind. All that I could do was to speak a few words of instruction and invitation from God's word and offer prayer. But he died as he had lived, and, so far as I know, without a ray of light.

I will not utter the fearful words of malignant rage that have fallen from human lips in dying moments. Some resist death as long as possible, and openly declare that they will not die. I have in remembrance the case of a comparatively young lawyer who almost defied death, and boldly proclaimed his determination to live.

I have known a man to spend his last strength in trying to strike a Christian minister who strove to lead him to Christ. A young woman of high social position and many accomplishments utterly refused all the offices of a kind pastor, under the awful conviction that she had destroyed her own soul; and she gave utterance in her last hours to the direst hatred of the blessed Redeemer.

Francesco Speira professed the evangelical faith in the days of the Reformation under Luther; but he afterward abjured it, and became the prey of remorseful despair until he died. The intolerable conviction that he was for ever lost caused him at times to roar like a beast, and yet in his despair he could not repent; and so he left the world.

Some of "the wicked have no bands in their death." They have their good things in this life, and make no provision for the life to come. Judging themselves as good as their neighbors, and better than some confessors of Christ, they die—regretfully, but not in despair, for God gives them strong delusions to believe a lie.

Others—and they are many—die in a moment, in the twinkling of an eye. They are on shipboard, and go down into the depths when the cyclone smites them; or on the cars in the wreck or the flames; or their hearts fail as they sit among their kindred or walk the streets or pursue their callings or their pleasures. And many fall in the deadly strife of arms, covered with martial glory, honored of men, but utterly destitute of holiness, without which no man shall see the Lord.

But there is a class of persons of whom I shall have something hopeful to say in the next lecture. They are in very close relation to the people of God. Children of the covenant, they have borne the sign and seal of the righteousness of faith from infancy. Or, if this is not the case, they belong to Christian households. From childhood they have been taught the truths of Scripture by believing parents and have been claimed for God. Coming to their death by sudden calamity or after short sickness, they deeply feel their need of Christ, and may not be classed with those who have no hope in their death.

I close this lecture with a delightful theme—the Death of the Righteous. "Precious in the sight of the Lord is the death of his saints."

Aaron died in Mt. Hor, and was gathered unto his people.

It was made the duty of Moses to go up into Mt. Nebo and die, and be gathered unto his people; but he was allowed first to see the good land that God was about to give to the children of Israel.

Stephen, the first Christian martyr, stood before the council that condemned him, and they saw his face as it had been the face of an angel. Cut to the heart by his words of truth, they gnashed on him with their teeth. "But he being full of the Holy Ghost, looked up steadfastly into heaven, and saw the glory of God, and Jesus standing on the right hand of God." As the stones smote him he called upon God and said, "Lord Jesus, receive my spirit." Even after this "he kneeled down and cried with a loud voice, Lord, lay not this sin to their charge. And when he had said this, he fell asleep." "He fell asleep"—language that our Saviour authorizes us to use in speaking of the Christian's decease. "Our friend Lazarus sleepeth, but I go that I may awake him out of sleep." And therefore St. Paul wrote, "If we believe that Jesus died and rose again, even so them also that sleep in Jesus will God bring with him."

In anticipation of his own martyrdom, Paul wrote these brave words to Timothy, his own son in the faith: "I am now ready to be offered, and the time of my departure is at hand. I have fought a good fight, I have finished my course, I have kept the faith: henceforth there is laid up for me a crown of righteousness, which the Lord, the righteous judge, shall give me at that day; and not to me only, but unto all them also that love his appearing."

POLYCARP, who died in the flames of martyrdom A. D. 155, is reported to have exclaimed, "O Father of thy beloved and blessed Son Jesus Christ! O God of all principalities and of all creation! I bless thee that thou hast counted me worthy of this day and this hour, to receive my portion in the number of the martyrs, in the cup of Christ."

JOHN OWEN, author of many standard works, and among them *The Person and Glory of Christ*, was born 1616, and died near London in 1683. "Oh, Brother Payne," he said, "the long-looked-for day is come at last, in which I shall see the glory in another manner than I have ever yet done or been capable of doing."

THOMAS HALYBURTON, professor of divinity in the University of St. Andrews, died there A. D.

1712. On his death-bed he testified, "Here is a demonstration of the reality of religion, that I, a poor, weak, timorous man, as much afraid of death as any, am now enabled, by the power of grace, composedly and with joy to look death in the face."

RICHARD CECIL, born 1748 and dying 1810, gave this testimony: "My first convictions on the subject of religion [he was once an infidel] were confirmed by observing that really religious persons had some solid happiness among them, which I felt the vanities of the world could not give. I shall never forget standing by the bedside of my sick mother. "Are you not afraid to die?" I asked. "No! no!" was her reply. "Why does the uncertainty of another life give you no concern?" I asked. She answered, "Because God has said, 'Fear not; when thou passest through the waters, I will be with thee; and through the rivers, they shall not overflow thee.'" He adds, "Let me die the death of the righteous."

JOHN WESLEY, the founder of Methodism (1703–1797), closed his long and useful life with these words: "The best of all is, God is with us."

THOMAS SCOTT (1747–1821), shortly before his departure, said, "This is heaven begun. I have done with darkness for ever, for ever. Satan is vanquished; nothing now remains but salvation with eternal glory."

MRS. ELIZABETH HARVEY, the wife of a missionary in Bombay, exclaimed, "If this is the dark valley, it has not a dark spot in it. All is light, light."

Wanting words to express her views of the majesty and glory of Christ, she added, "It seems that if all other glory were annihilated, and nothing left but his bare self, it would be enough; it would be a universe of glory."

So we are reminded of blessed RUTHERFORD'S words, in one of his charming letters: "Heaven and Christ are the same thing."

The testimony of Dr. EDWARD PAYSON (1783–1827) of Portland, Maine, is remarkable for its clearness, comprehensiveness and preciousness. Few persons, after living, as he did, in glad, sometimes melancholy, yet always intense devotion to the service of Christ and his Church and cause, are permitted to say much on the bed of death. Like his brother Henry, a ruling elder of our church when I became its pastor in 1850, he was of a nervous temperament, and suffered often from deep depression of spirit. Dr. Payson is said to have spoken thus at different times on his death-bed:

"My God is in this room. I see him, and oh, how lovely is the sight! How glorious does he appear! worthy of ten thousand hearts, if I had so many to give!"

At another time, when his body was racked with inconceivable pain, he exclaimed, as if returning from a field of conflict and victory, "The battle's fought! the battle's fought! and the victory is won; the victory is won for ever! I am going to bathe in an ocean of purity and benevolence and happiness to all eternity. . . . The celestial city is in full view; its glories beam upon me; its breezes fan me; its odors are wafted to me; its music strikes upon my ear, and its spirit breathes into my heart. Nothing separates me from it but the river of death, which now appears as a narrow rill which may be crossed at a single step whenever God shall give permission. . . . The Sun of righteousness has been drawing nearer and nearer, appearing larger and larger as he approached, and now he fills the hemisphere, pouring forth a flood of glory, in which I seem to float like an insect in the beams of the sun, exulting, yet almost trembling, while I gaze on excessive brightness, and wondering, with unutterable wonder, why God should deign thus to shine upon a sinful worm."

The Rev. Richard W. Dickinson, D. D., of Fordham, N. Y., with his family about him, looking heavenward and reaching out his arms as if to embrace the Saviour coming to receive him to himself, simply said, "My crucified and risen Lord!"

Mortimer Strong, a deacon of our church, raised himself up in the bed, and with firm voice and deepest emotion exclaimed,

"Lend, lend your wings. I mount, I fly.
O Death, where is thy sting? O Grave, where is thy victory?"

And, finally, the Rev. Charles Hodge, D D., whom so many of us knew and honored and loved, "seeing his widowed daughter weeping while she watched him, stretched his hand toward her and said, 'Why should you grieve, daughter? To be absent from the body is to be with the Lord; to be with the Lord is to see the Lord; to see the Lord is to be like him!'

"To a loving inquiry of his wife he once said, 'Yes, my love, my Saviour is with me every step of the way; but I am too weak to talk about it.' Once she asked him if it would comfort him if she should repeat aloud his favorite hymn. He answered, 'No, dearest; I am repeating it over and over again to myself all the while.'"

It was the hymn of Mrs. Weiss, daughter of the Archbishop of Dublin, composed on her death-bed.

I make record of the entire hymn as revealing the dying thoughts of the great and good man so long professor in this seminary:

Jesus, I am never weary
When upon this bed of pain;
If thy presence only cheer me,
All my loss I count but gain.
Ever near me,
Ever near me, Lord, remain!

Dear ones come with fruit and flowers,
Thus to cheer my heart the while,
In these deeply anxious hours.
Oh, if Jesus only smile!
Only Jesus
Can these trembling fears beguile.

All my sins were laid upon thee,
All my griefs were on thee laid;
For the blood of thine atonement
All my utmost debt has paid.
Dearest Saviour!
I believe, for thou hast said.

Dearest Saviour! go not from me;
Let thy presence still abide;
Look in tenderest love upon me:
I am sheltering at thy side.
Dearest Saviour!
Who for suffering sinners died.

Both mine arms are clasped around thee,
  And my head is on thy breast,
And my weary soul has found thee
  Such a *perfect*, *perfect* rest.
    Dearest Saviour!
  Now I know that I am blessed.

LECTURE II.

Salvation Possible, and in many cases Probable, on the Death-Bed.

LECTURE II.

SALVATION POSSIBLE, AND IN MANY CASES PROBABLE, ON THE DEATH-BED.

AT first thought it may seem to be a waste of time to state and prove what none holding to the truth of Scripture will deny. But there are some—I hope not many—who have no controlling belief that the lost may be found and saved in the last hours of a sinful and wasted life. A Christian pastor told me that his experience with many who professed to find Christ as their Saviour, or promised amendment of life if God would spare them, while on beds of sickness, and afterward recovered, was so disheartening that he had ceased to make special efforts for the salvation of the sick. A very sad mistake! Worse than a mistake! While there is life there is hope. James M. Campbell, in his little book, *Unto the Uttermost*, has well said of the Christian ambassador, "Down to the dying moment he is to stand beside the sinner, telling of the mercy that stoops to receive the fragments of a wasted life; telling of the blood of sprinkling, and challenging earth and hell to show a sin it cannot cleanse." *

The difference between recovering from sickness to prove one's profession false, and dying possibly to prove it true, we have already seen, is too great for the human mind to compass.

There are two extremes, to one or other of which we tend in relation to those for whose souls we watch, especially when the circumstances are peculiarly trying: one is *presumption*, and the other *despair*. And to one or other of these extremes the unsaved are in danger of being driven in times of severe and deadly sickness.

"Men of the world," as we are wont to call them, busy with the affairs, the ambitions, the pleasures of this life, if they allow themselves to think seriously of the life to come, hope to have leisure and disposition to prepare for that other life when they have achieved success or when the solemnities of the last sickness are upon and around them. This is *presumption*.

When the leisure of retirement from active business is theirs, the disposition and ability for the mightiest of all human enterprises, the laying hold

* The book carefully read is helpful; but there is much in it I cannot receive as true.

of eternal life, are seldom given them. And when sickness comes, with its pains and exhaustion, its distraction and fear of death, the necessity of submitting to medical treatment, and, it may be, the careful exclusion from their presence of all who would speak to them of Christ and the great salvation,—if they retain reason and consciousness they begin to recognize the difficulties in their way, and may go to the other extreme, sinking into hopeless despondency, the sinful *despair* of unbelief.

While not forgetting that the general drift of Bible teaching and divine providence, with the main facts of human experience, is strongly against the delay of conversion until sickness comes, we should fortify ourselves with strong reasons for believing that conversion, and therefore salvation, is possible when death is near.

1. One of these reasons is the nature of conversion.

I use the word "conversion" in the popular sense, as including the regeneration of the sinner by the Holy Spirit, and his consequent turning unto God through Jesus Christ. In this view it comprehends effectual calling, faith in at least its first act of looking unto Jesus, and repentance, the two graces last named rooting themselves in the first.

The Westminster Assembly's Shorter Catechism is helpful here, for its definitions are not only Scriptural, but clear as crystal, and they set no limit to the saving power of the Holy Spirit while the earthly life continues:

"Effectual calling is the work of God's Spirit, whereby, convincing us of our sin and misery, enlightening our minds in the knowledge of Christ, and renewing our wills, he doth persuade and enable us to embrace Jesus Christ, freely offered to us in the gospel."

"Faith in Jesus Christ is a saving grace, whereby we receive and rest upon him alone for salvation, as he is offered to us in the gospel."

"Repentance unto life is a saving grace, whereby a sinner, out of a true sense of his sin, and apprehension of the mercy of God in Christ, doth, with grief and hatred of his sin, turn from it unto God, with full purpose of, and endeavor after, new obedience."

Rarely as this may be thought to occur, it is quite within the power of the Holy Spirit and the grace of God on a death-bed. The effectual calling or the new creation of a lost sinner is always, we believe, the instantaneous work of the Holy Spirit. Saving faith and repentance follow. The sinner is passive in the birth from above. He may have in his mind and heart the word of God as the instrument by means of which the work is effected, and yet not know when or how the great change is wrought. "The wind bloweth where it listeth, and thou hearest the sound thereof, but canst not tell whence it cometh and whither it goeth; so is every one that is born of the Spirit."

Even if a sinner on his death-bed is indifferent or presumptuous or despairing, others who love his soul may be prayerful and importunate in seeking his salvation. In that case it may please God that the blessing shall come as to the paralytic borne by others and laid at the feet of Jesus for healing.

If you are ministering to the sufferer, you may be gratefully surprised to see the proofs of the Holy Spirit's presence and saving power in his agitation, in his new views of sin and righteousness and judgment; in his sorrow for his sinfulness and transgressions, of which, at last, he has begun to take account as in God's presence; in his confession, his godly sorrow, his prayer for pardon and his humble and glad reliance upon Christ as his Saviour and Master. The agitation of the trees of the wood and the lifting up of the great waves of the sea are not stronger proof that the winds are abroad than such changes in a sinner are proof that the Holy Spirit has begun the work of his salvation. And we ought to be quick to recognize the work for which we have wrought earnestly with God and faithfully with man.

The analogy of all creative acts of which we have any knowledge strengthens our belief that the beginning of this saving work is instantaneous. "God spake and it was done; he commanded and it stood fast." He said, "Let light be," and light was. And as if on purpose to associate the two creative acts in our minds, we have the words of the Holy Spirit by the Apostle: "God, who commanded the light to shine out of darkness, hath shined in our hearts to give the light of the knowledge of the glory of God in the face of Jesus Christ." The principle of the new life is given to the sinner, dead in trespasses and sins, by the Spirit of God and in the use of some portion of the word of reconciliation. Whether the earthly life after that is measured by years or moments, salvation is sure. All else follows in a revealed and, so far as we know, a changeless order. "Whom he did predestinate, them he also called; and whom he called, them he also justified; and whom he justified, them he also glorified." Justification, adoption and sanctification are the fruitage of regeneration. They come as the blade, the ear and the full corn in the ear from the precious seed which God quickens to a plenteous harvest.

The process may be miraculously, and of course graciously, quick, reminding us how easily and instantly, in one case, by the will and word of Jesus, water was converted into the best of wine. In all ordinary cases there must be the vine, the fruitful season, the leaf, the blossom, the clusters of juicy grapes, the wine-press or the treading of feet, the wine-vat, the wine-cellar and the long years before the water becomes the beverage that men thirst for and enjoy.

2. There are well-authenticated cases of conversion with death in immediate prospect, but averted at the last moment, and giving the convert the privilege of bearing witness for himself.

I have long been familiar with a well-authenticated case of this kind. A young man from the city of New York was lost overboard in the Gulf of Mexico. Sinking beneath the waters, he soon became unconscious, and in that condition was rescued and after a time resuscitated. The account he gave on coming back to life, and afterward, was of great interest as bearing upon this point.

During the moments that passed before he lost consciousness he had many and momentous thoughts. Their multitude was the measure of time. Moments seemed to be lengthened to hours, until at last he appeared to himself to die. But in those swift moments he had time to review his life. A deep conviction of his ruin and helplessness as a justly-condemned sinner was the result. But he saw with equal clearness the open door of hope. It pleased God, as he believed, to reveal to him the way of life through Jesus Christ, and to enable him to take the first steps therein. He had been taught the great truths of the gospel before, but had never received them as a revelation and conveyance of life to himself. Now they became his by the teaching and gift of the Holy Spirit. He consciously received Jesus Christ as his Saviour and Master for the little remnant of his life and the eternity that was before him.

Happily, the companions of this young man were quickly directed to the spot where he lay. Restored to consciousness, he found himself, as he hoped, a new creature in Christ Jesus. He retained a vivid remembrance of the covenant he had made with God with death in view, and faithfully performed his vow. Returning to his home in New York, he openly confessed Christ, who sought and, he believed, found him when doubly lost. Years of sincere devotion gave pleasing evidence of the reality of the change, and he departed at last in the blessed hope of the life everlasting.

There is one case of conversion shortly before death, the record of which is preserved in the New Testament. Regarding this, therefore, there can be no doubt. But I call in question the warrant for the inference that there is only one, lest we should believe in death-bed conversions. As well infer, because there are few records in the Scriptures of triumphant departures, that the saints of old did not in many cases close life in peace and joy. Better adopt the view of Augustine, that "There is one instance of death-bed repentance recorded in the Scriptures—the penitent thief—that none should despair; and only one, that none may presume."

I believe that in the aggregate there are many instances of salvation coming to sinners on beds of death, and that God will graciously own pastoral wisdom and fidelity to the large increase of the number.

The case referred to by Augustine, in language often quoted, has special claims upon our thought.

I share in the wonder and gratitude of those who have made it a careful study, and trust you will pardon my lingering upon it a little, even though I have nothing new to say.

"With Jesus our Lord two thieves (*λῃσταὶ*, robbers) were crucified, one on the right hand, and another on the left." Each of the four gospels makes record of the fact, yet no two in precisely the same words.*

The "disciple whom Jesus loved" contents himself with the simple but affecting record: "And two others with him, on either side one, and Jesus in the midst."

The Evangelist Luke alone twice calls them malefactors (*κακοῦργοι*, evil-workers). The arrangement of the three crosses and their victims was a device of the haters of Jesus to put upon him the greater shame. They had no thought of fulfilling prophecy in thus literally numbering him with transgressors, and of preparing the way for a most wonderful work of saving grace. The enemies of God and man often defeat themselves by choosing their own way. Never before had such a scene been witnessed in Golgotha. It cannot be repeat-

* Matt. 27:44; Mark 15:27; Luke 23:32, 39-43; John 19:18.

ed. The central cross was the cynosure of all eyes. It bore the Lord of glory—the Son of God, made the Son of man—that the sons and daughters of men might become the sons and daughters of the Lord Almighty. And these were the hours of his greatest weakness, shame and anguish of spirit.

It seems incredible that in these solemn and awful hours the people whom he had served in many ways should revile him; that even the chief priests and scribes and elders should invent terms of reproach and blasphemy; and, strangest of all, that the thieves also which were crucified with him should cast the same in his teeth. But such is the testimony of the writers of the first two gospels.

What a treasure, therefore, is the third synoptic gospel, that gives the final fact regarding one of the malefactors! It is Luke, called elsewhere "the beloved physician," who makes the record to which I refer, in these impressive words: "And one of the malefactors which were hanged railed on him, saying, If thou be the Christ, save thyself and us. But the other, answering, rebuked him, saying, Dost not thou fear God, seeing thou art in the same condemnation? And we indeed justly, for we receive the due reward of our deeds; but this man hath done nothing amiss. And he said unto

Jesus, Lord, remember me when thou comest into (in) thy kingdom. And Jesus said unto him, Verily I say unto thee, To-day shalt thou be with me in paradise."

This is the record entire. This man felt the pangs of true grief for his sins in the very presence of the crucified Jesus. The fear of God fell upon him. He acknowledged the justice of his condemnation under human law and his deep guilt under God's law. He felt most keenly that because he was a criminal in relation to men he was a sinner in relation to God. Wronging his fellows, he had offended God. Gladly would he have led his fellow-criminal to repentance, confession and prayer, but he tried in vain. Wonderful change! The Holy Spirit was his teacher. No voice of his fellow-men helped him. Pitiful women stood afar off beholding, but their eyes and thoughts were on their expiring Lord. Only Christ himself answered him. And what an answer! It was better than a coronation. "To-day shalt thou be with me in paradise." We do not know that any other words than those already quoted passed between them. But they were enough. They did not overtax even a dying man. The remaining hours of his mortal agony, we suppose, were spent in looking unto

Jesus, listening to the gracious words that fell from his lips, beholding him as he gave up the ghost, and then waiting till death should set him free to join his Lord and Saviour in the paradise of God. One such case is enough. It compels the belief that the salvation of the lost is possible on the bed of death. It demands of us the recognition of this possibility in the most desperate cases. Better speak words of life in the ear that seems closed for ever than be silent when an immortal soul is in peril. I once read short portions of Scripture and prayed in few words at the bedside of a man who could not see nor speak nor move, and continued to do so, visiting him day after day, when he was thought to be unconscious and quite beyond all helpful ministry. But he rallied at last, remembered every interview, heard and considered all that was read and spoken to him and the prayers offered, and was thankful for the effort made in his behalf. He did not recover from his sickness, but he had hope in his death, and we shared with his kindred in the belief that he died in the Lord.

Still, it is not wise or safe to wait for a last sickness for opportunities to win souls to Christ. I cannot forget the impressive words of the Rev. Dr.

Spencer in the last of three published sermons on "The Delay of Conversion."

"I must confess to you," he says, "that I can think of no words, form or figure to express the diminutiveness of that hope with which we preach the gospel to the graceless on their beds of death. What becomes of those who die we know not—thank God, we know not. But among all the instances of supposed conversion on a sick-bed which I have known (and I have known many in a ministry of twenty-five years), only four of those who recovered gave any evidence in after-life of the religion which they thought they had gained when sick. . . . What a lesson on the delay of conversion! What an appalling lesson!" Then he enlarges on the difficulties and dangers of those who come to their last sickness without a well-tried hope in Christ.

Let the great lesson of these strong sermons remain. They are the testimony of a great and good man—one of the most faithful and successful pastors I have ever known. But in passing to the other part of our subject, viz. *Salvation Probable on a Death-Bed* in certain cases, I cannot withhold the suggestion that the difference between a sick-bed and a death-bed is not recognized as it should be. It does not follow, as a known truth, because so large a proportion of those who think they have found Christ on a sick-bed, on recovering find themselves mistaken, that a like proportion of those who say for the first time on their death-bed that he is all their salvation and all their desire are mistaken too.

The conversion of the jailer of Philippi occurred in very close relation to death threatened by his own hand. But there is another feature of his case that deserves notice in this connection. It is said of him that after receiving the answer to his question, "Sirs, what must I do to be saved?"—"Believe on the Lord Jesus Christ, and thou shalt be saved and thy house," he took Paul and Silas, "the same hour of the night, and washed their stripes; and was baptized, he and all his, straightway."

Already Lydia and her household had been baptized.

In one other case we have the Apostle's testimony, "I baptized also the household of Stephanas." Here, therefore, were these households brought into covenant relations with God, and baptized in visible recognition and token of the relation. I am not now assuming that there were young children in all or any of these families, and consequently pleading for infant baptism. It rests upon firmer ground than this. It is enough to claim that in these three cases the household covenant was kept clearly in view. It was as dear to St. Paul, a converted Jew and the founder of many Christian churches, as to Simon Peter, who, on the day of Pentecost, said, "The promise is unto you and to your children, and to all that are afar off, even as many as the Lord our God shall call." And it was no dearer to him than to the prophet Joel, eight hundred, and to Abraham, nineteen hundred, years before Christ. That old covenant stands in all the fullness of its benediction for parents and their children and children's children to this day. Even the Decalogue, in its second commandment, reveals God as "showing mercy unto thousands of them that love him and keep his commandments." And these "thousands" we believe are generations.

The covenant with Abraham was partly in these words: "And I will establish my covenant between me and thee, and thy seed after thee, in their generations, for an everlasting covenant, to be a God unto thee, and to thy seed after thee."

When, therefore, the salvation of God comes to the head of a house, a blessing is diffused through the household. In by far the larger portion of the

Christian Church the younger members of a family receive the sign and seal of the righteousness of faith in holy baptism when the older believe the gospel. And whether the baptism come to adults or infants, it has precisely the same meaning: "Baptism is a sacrament, wherein the washing with water in the name of the Father, and of the Son, and of the Holy Ghost, doth signify and seal our engrafting into Christ, and partaking of the benefits of the covenant of grace, and our engagement to be the Lord's."

Hundreds and thousands of children and youths and adults the world over bear this sacred seal on their persons. Many have come to years of full responsibility without meeting the engagement to be the Lord's which their parents made for them at their baptism. They may fall sick and die as well as others. We do not forget that the household covenant is not unconditional. Eli and Samuel and Aaron and David had sons who departed far from God, and so far as we know they died in their sins. But the privileges of parents under the former dispensation are not denied to parents under this. The advantage is with the new and latter until the Lord shall come.

Here, I think, is laid a broad and deep foundation for the hope that many children of the covenant are saved by grace in their last hours. The Rev. James W. Alexander, D. D., in his *Plain Words to a Young Communicant*, expresses the opinion that in the trying circumstances of a last sickness not a few are thrown back upon what he calls "the faith of their childhood," and, coming to the consciousness of need, find it all supplied in Jesus Christ.

I fully believe, whatever exceptions there may be, that salvation flows as a river, broad and deep, in the channel of the household covenant.

1. In some cases—many, we may hope—the change is wrought in very early life, though not clearly recognized by parents and friends. Or they may be surprised now and then with almost unconscious acts on the part of their children, compelling the thought that the fear and love of God have been planted in their hearts.

Suddenly fatal sickness falls upon them, and death is at hand, but there is no slavish fear. They assure those who care tenderly for their salvation that they can remember no time when they did not love and trust the Saviour and desire to please him. They have never been prayerless. It has long been their wish to confess Jesus as their

Saviour, and it has grieved them not to come to the Lord's table with his people. But they have been kept from it in accordance with a custom that has not favored early admission to it—a custom, I believe, more hurtful than helpful to the young, the household and the Church. Nor can I think it pleasing to the Saviour. No one doubts, when children of this class have departed this life, that they have gone to be for ever with the Lord. Surely the terms of admission to the Church triumphant must suffice for admission to communion with the Saviour's disciples on earth.

I cannot withhold, in this connection, a few words from the last sermon delivered to his own people in the Metropolitan Tabernacle, by the Rev. Charles H. Spurgeon, on the morning of June 7, 1891. The very next day he had the chill which was the beginning of his fatal sickness.

He was speaking on the words, "And his men that were with him did David bring up (to Hebron), every man *with his household.*" His words are all the more suggestive because he was a Baptist.

"There is a Hebron," he said, "where Jesus reigns as anointed king, and he will not be there and leave one of us behind. His poor people who have been with him in faintness and weariness shall be with him in glory, *and their households.* Hold on to that additional blessing. I pray you, hold on to it. Do not let slip the words *and their households.* I fear we often lose a blessing on our households through clipping the promises. When the jailer asked what he must do to be saved, what was the answer? 'Believe on the Lord Jesus Christ and thou shalt be saved.' You have heard that answer hundreds of times, have you not? Did you ever hear the rest of it? Why do preachers and quoters snip off corners from gospel promises? It runs thus: 'Thou shalt be saved and thy house.' Lay hold of that blessed enlargement of grace."

Shall we that believe in the household covenant have painful doubts as to the salvation of our children who die without fear and claiming the Saviour as their own?

2. In many cases the change from death unto life manifestly has not been wrought by the Holy Spirit up to the time of the last sickness. The folly of youth has continued. A wayward spirit in relation to parental authority and the restraints of the school and the church may have been dominant, and even defiant. They have been taught the truths of God's word in the home, the sanc-

tuary, the Sunday-school and, it may be, the college. Prayer has been offered for them continually by parents, kindred, pastors, teachers, churches, and by many, too, who may have gone before into the heavens. At last they are arrested by fatal sickness. The Saviour's will and hand are in the arrest. He stands at the door and knocks. Is he less concerned to save than we are? less than Satan is to destroy? He sends his messengers to them. Is there no sign of his willingness to save in this? By his word and Spirit he shows to many the plague of their hearts and constrains them to ask for the healing of the plague. Conscience at last is fully aroused. There is recollection, sorrow, confession, inquiry, What must I do to be saved? It is the old question. And the old answer is the true one—the whole of it, because it brings to view the household covenant: "Believe on the Lord Jesus Christ, and thou shalt be saved and thy house." Parental faith comes to the rescue. Covenant blessings are importunately sought. The God of salvation hears for Christ's sake. He is not watching to kill, but to make alive. The wonders of salvation are all his, and bring glory to his name. The time element does not mean so much to him as to us. William Jay once said that

Christ is able "to save to the uttermost ends of the earth; to the uttermost limits of time; to the uttermost period of life; to the uttermost depth of depravity; to the uttermost depth of misery; and to the uttermost measure of perfection." And Spurgeon, quoted by the same writer (James M. Campbell), says: "If you are so far gone that there seems to be not even a ghost of a shade of a shadow of a hope anywhere about you, yet if you believe in Jesus you shall live. Trust in the Lord Jesus Christ, for he is worthy to be trusted. Throw yourself upon him, and he will carry you in his bosom. Cast your whole weight upon his atonement; it will bear the strain."

This sweet truth, tenderly reiterated in the ear of the dying who have long neglected it, may be blessed of God to moving their sorrow for him whom they have pierced, and their joy that he waits to be gracious, and is willing and able to save them in their last hours.

If any pervert the truth that sinners are saved even in such circumstances, and therefore continue to neglect the great salvation in time of health, delaying conversion for the time of sickness, they have reason to fear that when at last they call, if ever they do, God will not answer.

Will you pardon an allusion to a personal incident? It had much to do with correcting what up to that time had been, I think, a false estimate of my own with regard to responsibility for the perversion of facts as to death-bed repentance, especially when published to the world.

Being in London, England, in the fall of 1858, I was invited to address the Young Men's Christian Association. About six hundred were present, many of them not disciples of Christ. In urging them to embrace the gospel without delay, I related the leading facts in regard to a young man of promise in the office of the Atlantic Mutual Insurance Company of New York City, who was fatally hurt one Saturday night, and, after seven days and seven nights of unutterable agony, died in the peace which only the gospel can give. As I was with him more or less all through that eventful week, and after every interview made careful record of his words and changing experiences, and also wrote letters to him instructing him in the truths of the gospel and the way of salvation, to be read to him by his mother when, for any reason, I could not see him, I was able from memory and heart to give the diary of that wonderful week. Especially I related how, from my first interview with him, on Monday, July 20, 1857, until Wednesday morning, the 22d, he said strongly that he was "not prepared for death, and knew that he was a lost soul, and deserved to be lost, because, while he knew his duty, he would not mind God."

But the story is quite too long to relate here. Let it be enough to add that on the afternoon of that day, Wednesday, July 22d, he greeted me with the glad tidings that he had found peace in believing. He gave a most satisfactory account of the change, and good reasons for the hope that was in him. Nor did it afterward fail—except during two or three dark hours, from which he emerged into the clear light of an endless day—as all who knew him best believed.

On the platform, as I gave the narrative, was the Rev. T. W. J. Wylie, D. D., of Philadelphia, Pa., then a stranger to me. Deeply affected, even to tears, he accompanied me to my hotel, and urged me to publish the account which I had given orally. I told him that while I could easily do it, as my notes were full and consecutive, yet I had not thought of doing it. I had no question, nor had others who knew the facts, as to the reality and blessedness of the change, but I was afraid the living might pervert the lateness of the conversion to their own delay in seeking the Saviour, and die in their sins. Dr. Wylie reasoned earnestly with me. He said the unsaved perverted even the gospel. I had all the facts. I could not be held responsible for the perversion of them by others, but I would be responsible if I withheld them from the knowledge of others, and so virtually suppressed them.

I promised to consider what he said, and finally I acted upon his suggestion, and the Carters in New York and houses in London and Edinburgh published the narrative. A year or two ago the Messrs. Carter gave the stereotype plates to me, and I gave them to the Board of Publication. Under a slightly changed name, *Saved by Grace; or, The Last Week in the Life of Davis Johnson, Jr.*, it is now published by the Board, and I am thankful to know that it has not lived so long in vain.

I ought to add that the young man was the son of Christian parents. His father had been for many years an elder in a Reformed (Dutch) church, though at the time a member of our church, and the son was taught the Scriptures from his youth.

3. But the children of godly parents may be cut off more suddenly still.

Some years ago I was called to visit a young Scotchman, not long in this country, who had taken employment for the time in a distillery. Caught in the machinery, he was so fearfully torn that he lived but a few hours. Far away in the old country, his believing father and mother knew nothing of his hurt until, a few days later, I wrote them of his death. Up to the time of his fatal injury he had made no confession of Christ as his Saviour. He had been baptized in infancy on the faith of his parents. Well instructed in the Scriptures and familiar with the Assembly's Shorter Catechism, much precious truth was in his memory. Under the help given him by the Holy Spirit, the truth seemed to find its way at once to his heart. He acknowledged his sinfulness, transgressions and guilt. Of a quick understanding in the fear of the Lord, he was eager for instruction, receiving the truth in the love of it, and accepting Christ as his Saviour with all readiness and gladness of heart. It was a sacred pleasure to stay by him, leading him Christward and heavenward, although the throbbing of his failing heart could be seen through the opening the cogs had made.

4. Many sons are sent or go from their Christian homes never to return, and yet to be found, as I trust this young man will be, safe in the Father's house at the home-coming of the godly parents.

Overtaken on the sea or the land by sickness or calamity, they are suddenly confronted with death, are thrown back upon their childhood's instruction, and, by the watchful Spirit of God, come to a better than even their childhood's faith. The loving Saviour, quick and eager to find his erring ones, meets them in the person of some faithful messenger, a Christian fellow-sailor or soldier or chaplain, and draws them to himself, it may be amid the terrors of the shipwreck or the battle-field. Shall the suddenness of their departure deprive him of his purchased rights, or kindred and friends of strong consolation? The water does not drown nor the bullet strike them without the knowledge and will of the living Christ. Quicker even than water drowns or a bullet flies the Holy Spirit may give life to an instructed soul.

5. There is a class of the children of the covenant who live in sad estrangement from Christ till they are not only mature in years, but some of them past the meridian of life. They may be restrained by education, by conscience, by all the influences of Christian homes, from outbreaking wickedness, and yet have no knowledge of the plague of their own hearts. Or they may break loose from all restraints, and, like the prodigal, follow the desires

and devices of their own hearts until confronted by death and compelled to consider their ways.

Some years ago I was asked to visit a young woman, the child of a believing mother who had entered into rest. The daughter had attempted to take her own life under the impression that she had committed the sin that hath never forgiveness.

She was caught in the very act and carefully guarded by day and night. When convinced that she had not committed the sin, the nature of which she did not know, and that it would be a most foolish, cowardly and wicked thing to take her own life, she gave me her promise that she would not attempt it again. And when told plainly that, although she had not committed that sin, she had sinned far more deeply than she knew, but not more deeply than the Saviour knew, she was enabled to cast herself as she was upon him, and to accept his grace and blood, even himself, as all her salvation and all her desire. That was the beginning of a happy and useful Christian life which continues to this day.

A young man who was carefully reared in a Christian home was impelled by an uncontrollable passion to go to sea. With the consent of his parents, he embarked on a whale-ship bound for the

South Atlantic. The Bible given by his mother, with the request that he would read it daily, was in his chest, and up to the time of which I have occasion to speak had been used but little if at all. He was a sailor among sailors, and lived as he pleased, though happily there was a Christian shipmate in the crew.

After a prosperous voyage the ship was about to return to the North, and he was greatly elated with the near prospect of seeing his parents and revisiting the scenes and companions of his early years having tales of travel and adventure to tell. But in stowing down the oil when the sea was rough a sudden lurch of the vessel brought a cask of oil against him with such force that both his legs were crushed and he received other injuries that soon proved fatal. He knew from the first that he could not live. His Christian shipmate at once shared the deep concern he felt for his salvation. He was sent to the chest for the long-neglected Bible, and asked to read where it told how to get ready for death and heaven. He turned to the fifty-first Psalm, and, coming to the 10th verse, "Create in me a clean heart, O God, and renew a right spirit within me," he was requested to "hold there." "That is just what I want," said the dying sailor. "How shall I get it?" "Pray God to give it for Christ's sake," was the answer. "Oh, yes," the other exclaimed; "Jesus is the Saviour." —"Shipmate, it is an awful thing to die, and I've got to go. Oh, if mother was here to tell me how to get ready!" and he trembled with emotion. After a short pause, in which he seemed to be in deep thought, he said, "Do you know of any place where it is said that such sinners as I can be saved?" The words, "This is a faithful saying, and worthy of all acceptation, that Christ Jesus came into the world to save sinners, of whom I am chief," and "He is able to save them to the uttermost that come unto God by him, seeing he ever liveth to make intercession for them," were read. "That's plain," he said. "Now, if I only knew how to come to God!" "Come as a child to a father," was the answer. "How's that?" he asked. —"As the child feels that his father can help him in danger, so you are to feel that God can help you now. And as the child trusts his father by fleeing to him, so you must trust Jesus by casting yourself upon him." He lay a little while engaged in earnest pleading with God, as was evident from the few words that were overheard. Then the tears began to run down his face and a bright smile played like a sunbeam on his features. "He forgives me, and I shall be saved," he said with great sweetness of voice and manner. And as death came he said, "*He's come! he's come!*" "Who has come?" asked his shipmate. "Jesus has come," he whispered; and so his life here came to an end.

I will not doubt that the compassionate Saviour revealed himself to this poor sinner in the little interval between the hurt and the dying. Surely our compassion is not greater than his.

What reason can any one give for assuming that a man in such distressing circumstances, earnestly desiring to find the way of life, confessing himself a sinner and pleading for pardon and acceptance with God for Jesus' sake, must be deceived? Better a thousand times believe that the Saviour is at the door; that he has arranged all the circumstances for arresting and saving one that was lost; that the Holy Spirit waits for some lover of the truth to give voice to his saving word; that you are yourself the very person, if the providence of God our Saviour points to you; and that holy angels are ready to carry the ransomed soul to the opening heavens.

At the communion of the church of which I am

the senior pastor, held June 20, 1852, of the fourteen persons recognized as having been received by the Session, one was a young girl sixteen years old, now the devoted wife of a Christian minister and the mother of Christian children; another was a woman more than seventy years of age. Although the widow of a deacon, she had never known real soul-trouble for her sins until a few weeks before. Looking from her window at an early hour one morning, she saw an aged couple whom she knew well on their way to a meeting that was to be held in our prayer-room. She instantly felt a deep concern for her salvation. On the next Lord's day she was in her place in the house of God. I knew nothing of her anxiety. The text was "Quench not the Spirit." She thought the sermon was prepared for her. After a fortnight of deep heart-searching and most agonizing conviction of sin, she found the Saviour, and great peace in believing. A few months later she fell in a street of New York, was carried to the house of a friend, and died, broken in body, but healed by the blood and touch of Christ, a joyful witness to the last of the power and preciousness of saving grace.

I have mentioned her case because it shows the patience, the compassion and the fixed purpose with which the Saviour keeps watch over individual souls, and surpasses and surprises us in saving some whom we might pass by as hardly responsive to any influence of truth by which others are won to Christ. Death-bed repentances of younger persons are not more wonderful, and they are not limited to the children or descendants of Christian parents.

I close this lecture by giving somewhat in detail an incident that I often recall with tender interest and cannot forget while life lasts:

Through the whole history of South Third Street Presbyterian Church, Brooklyn, N. Y., the prayer-meeting following the communion has been devoted especially to parents and their children, though we commonly include Sunday-school teachers and their scholars.

Knowing that the Rev. Nathaniel Hewitt, D. D., pastor of the Presbyterian church in Bridgeport, Ct., was the guest of one of our elders who lived not far from the place of meeting, I hastened to the house and asked him to be present and make an address. He would not promise to do so, as he was in one of his melancholy moods. He told me to go on with the service, and that if he came it would be quite late. And, sure enough, he came in while I was speaking to the people. He was tall and large (I had almost said immense, for he had a most impressive presence) and deeply solemn, wearing on this occasion a fur muffler high around his neck and face, for the weather was cold. It was evident that he was deeply affected by the sight that met his eyes on entering the place—a large lecture-room full of parents and their offspring, teachers and their scholars. He did not decline the place that I at once offered him in the pulpit. Without removing overcoat or muffler he began with these very words:

"This is a great subject, a very great subject—the Supremacy of God in the Family." Continuing, he said that the children of Christian households sometimes pursued a violent course in relation to God, and he pursued a violent course toward them. In illustration of this, he stated that during the war of 1812–15 he was pastor of a church in Plattsburgh on Lake Champlain. On one occasion General Macomb, who was in command of the American forces stationed there, sent for him, that he might visit and instruct twenty-four soldiers who for serious offences had been tried and condemned to be shot. Six were to suffer the extreme penalty of the law the following day. The others, though they knew it not, would be reprieved.

On his mournful errand he went to the guard-house, and from a list furnished him read the names of all the condemned men. All answered to their names and came forward with the exception of one, a man of high social position but of desperate character. He refused to leave his bunk. With the others Mr. Hewitt spent several hours, reading suitable portions of Scripture, preaching the gospel and offering fervent prayer that they might be saved. Late in the night he left them, returning the next morning early to his work of mercy. As he tenderly addressed them man by man, not yet knowing who were to live and who to die, he came at last to a Scotchman named Alexander. This man welcomed Mr. Hewitt with joy, and at once related the experience of the night and, briefly, his career from boyhood. On retiring to his place of rest he had been confronted with the sins of his whole life. Sleep fled. He remembered with deepest sorrow and pain his wayward conduct from his youth. He was a child of godly parents and many prayers. The very words of his father's intercessions in his behalf at the family altar came clearly to his mind. He recalled the answers to questions in the Shorter Catechism, and many portions of Scripture. From all the love and restraints of his home he secretly fled at the age of thirteen years, and for more than twenty years he had been a wanderer and vagabond on the face of the earth and on the sea. At last he had been suddenly and justly arrested by the strong arm of military authority and power. During the night just past he saw the utter ruin in which he was involved as a criminal under human law, a transgressor under God's law, and now condemned, without reprieve, to die an ignominious death; for he had learned this.

But the discovery of his helpless ruin was accompanied by another, equally clear. He saw the way of life through Jesus Christ. He saw plainly that the glory of Christ's person and offices and work answered to the deformity and guilt of his person and life. He was looking unto Jesus, clinging to him as his Saviour, and awaiting without fear the moment of his execution.

Mr. Hewitt was greatly moved in recognition of the matchless grace and power of the Saviour in relation to this sinful child of the covenant. Calling the other five men, who were at last made known to him as about to die, he gave them instruction suited to their sad condition, and told them of the grace of God in Alexander's case, entreating them to trust in the same Saviour. While thus engaged he felt something fall on his ear and neck, and, looking up to see what it was, he found one of the officers standing a little above him, weeping. And in that moment of silence the officer, tenderly addressing Alexander, begged him, if he could die peacefully and in hope of eternal life, to look up into his face and smile. He instantly gave the sign of inward peace and hope. Shortly after, the quick firing of a platoon of soldiers dismissed him, as Mr. Hewitt believed, to his Saviour's presence.

Some years later Mr. Hewitt was traveling in Vermont, and, having occasion to pass through a toll-gate, was accosted by the keeper with the question, "Sir, were you not the minister at Plattsburg during the last war?" Learning that he was, the gate-keeper stated that he was one of the eighteen soldiers condemned to die, but reprieved, yet during all that awful night expecting to be shot in the morning. The instruction then given had been owned of God to his conversion.

Have you a doubt, dear brethren, that salvation is possible on a death-bed? and that in some cases it is probable, and even more than probable? Imperfect as the argument of this lecture has been, I sincerely hope that in your own ministry you may have the joy of winning many souls, and that you may despair of none while life lasts. I can speak confidently of one thing: when you have taken the soul of another upon your soul shortly before it leaves the world, and thought of its worth, felt its danger, prayed for it, and, as you believe, by God's blessing upon the truth won it to Christ, the all-sufficient Saviour, you will let no opportunity pass to give help to every other soul under your care that is ready to perish. There is exquisite, sacred joy in being used to voice the words of the silent Holy Spirit, and to make known in this way the present but unseen Saviour to one who needs nothing so much as to touch him by faith and be saved by his grace.

"They that be wise shall shine as the brightness of the firmament; and they that turn many to righteousness, as the stars for ever and ever."

LECTURE III.

Wrong Treatment of the Sick and Dying; Right Treatment of the Same; Uses that may be Properly Made of their Experience.

LECTURE III.

WRONG TREATMENT OF THE SICK AND DYING.

I DO not speak to you, gentlemen, as if you were preparing to be trained nurses, though that is a noble calling, and you may often do good service by wise suggestions as to the proper care of the body. But you are chiefly to watch for souls as they who must give account.

I refer mainly to the treatment of the sick and the dying, which, by God's blessing, may be their preparation for the life that remains to them here and the endless life of the future. The responsibility of their treatment is shared by physicians, ministers, kinsfolk, friends, and sometimes by paid nurses.

In critical cases it may not be easy to decide which of the two, the body or the soul, shall have the first care. We can reach the soul with saving truth only through the body. The Holy Spirit may use truth long before learned to reach and save the soul when we seem to be cut off from all access to a dying person by reason of his bodily condition. If the sickness is manifestly unto death and the patient has given no sign of vital union to Christ, the physician and friends should interpose no obstacle to wise efforts for the instruction and salvation of one so soon to know the great things of the other life. Everything should be made subordinate to this end.

1. And here, first, I have a word to say about physicians in their relation to persons who are very ill and may be near to death.

My own experience has been perhaps exceptionally pleasant, for the reason that I have been associated mainly with Christian men in the medical profession. They have welcomed me to fullest possible co-operation with themselves. Nothing but a hindrance that I recognized as real has kept me from the presence of their patients. I shall never forget the deep concern felt by Dr. Mason, formerly of Brooklyn, now, I have no doubt, in heaven, that one of his patients who had come to the bed of death might have a Christian hope before submitting to a very dangerous operation. Dr. Mason assured me that he would not proceed until he was satisfied, through me, that the sufferer had found rest and peace in Christ. And he shared in the great joy when I was permitted to say to him that

I believed his patient was ready for life or for instant death as the result of the proposed operation. It was not fatal, but it brought no relief, and he soon fell asleep in Jesus.

I cannot withhold here a reference to John Augustus McVicker, M. D., of New York City, who died in March, 1892, aged seventy-seven years. Dr. McVicker was for many years a devoted, earnest and leading member of St. George's Protestant Episcopal Church in Stuyvesant Square. Of him it was said that "besides his great skill as a physician for the body, he was also a born benefactor to the soul of every sufferer who came across his path. Morning, noon and night the Master's teachings were omnipotent with him."

In only one instance do I remember to have felt it my duty to administer reproof to a physician who attempted to restrict my attentions to a dying patient whom I thoroughly knew and who earnestly desired frequent and short interviews with me. The physician was a young man, and I told him plainly that I knew more of the sick-room than he did, and that I could not be controlled by what he had said. He had the good sense to apologize and to admit that he had made a mistake even with reference to his patient.

It is clear enough that unless a physician knows a minister to be wise in dealing with the sick—one who at once perceives what is helpful and what is hurtful—he must decline taking the responsibility of encouraging, or even permitting, his visits. He is waging a battle with disease. On the two sides in the conflict are life and death, and he is with the "life." Whether Christian or not, he ought to be intent on diagnosing the disease, watching symptoms, administering remedies and noting their effects. He may therefore quite forget that he is dealing with one who has yet to lay hold on eternal life while his grasp on the present life may be daily growing weaker. Or if he should recognize this sad condition of his patient, he may share a belief that is too common, that one who is distracted by the pains of the body and near to death is quite beyond the reach of salvation by faith in the Saviour. He ought to remember that what is impossible with men is possible with God; that while the sufferer is passing beyond his skill and beyond all remedial agents for the help of his body, he has not passed beyond the reach of Him who gave life to the dead. He should therefore gladly co-operate with ministers or others who wisely seek to point and lead the dying to Christ.

It is unspeakably sad when physicians who are in daily contact with the sick and dying have no care for human souls. After all, the healing of the body and its endless weal—for it shares the destiny of the soul—does not depend on human skill alone. It is said of Christ that "himself took our infirmities and bore our sicknesses." It is not wise nor right to make nothing of Christ while ministering to the body. Of Asa, one of the kings of Judah, it is said, "In his disease he sought not to the Lord, but to the physicians." Consequently the words follow immediately: "Asa slept with his fathers, and died in the one and fortieth year of his reign." I would not dare to reverse the order, putting the physician before the Lord. Looking unto the Lord and sending for the physician with faithful regard for his counsel will ensure the best results.

The physician in all ordinary cases has no more reason or right to exclude the minister, who seeks the salvation of the soul for eternity, and of the body with it, than has the minister to exclude the physician, who aims to heal the body for the few and uncertain years appointed it for life on the earth. And it may be well to repeat the belief which I share with many who are wise, that the word of God, and prayer ministered wisely, gently, sincerely by those who come to the sick in the name of the Lord, are among the most powerful of all remedial agencies. For nothing is more depressing to the sick than mental anguish, the tortures of an accusing conscience and the consequent fear of dying apart from Christ. On the other hand, the breathing of peace into a troubled soul and the hope of eternal life through Jesus Christ have, in well-attested cases, so quickened the restorative powers of nature as to turn the tide of sickness and prove the best possible help to the physician in bringing his patients back to health.

2. Pass now from physicians to others who are called to visit the sick and the dying. In our concern for their souls it is a great wrong to forget the weakness of their bodies. Often the powers of life are so far exhausted that anything more than the recital of an invitation or promise of the Scriptures and prayer in a few sentences, and all in a subdued voice, would be a cruelty and failure.

Some are weaker even than this. They may not be able to speak, and yet they show by signs which can be understood that they are not beyond the possibility of being reached by the word and Spirit of truth and life. To withhold a word in season and to refrain from offering audible prayer in such cases is to take a responsibility from which a true winner of souls may well shrink.

I have known instances where all the sensibilities of the body and the activities of the mind have seemed to be in suspense, and yet the sufferers were not known to have found rest in Christ. Not to have spoken plainly, as if sure of a hearing, would have been to lose the only opportunity likely to be given for seeking to save those who were ready to perish.

When the way is clear for repeated visits and free and full conversation, there is such a thing as disregarding the laws of the mind itself by presenting truth in other than the divine order and proportions. Haphazard work with the soul is worse than such work with the body, even as the life of the soul is more precious than the life of the body. We may mar if not thwart the work of the Holy Spirit by adopting methods not in keeping with those which he is wont to bless. As in revivals, so called, appeals to the emotions instead of instruction to the mind may produce effects which are mistaken for conversion, yet which soon come to naught, so an unwise counselor may deal with one sick unto death. He may calm his fears and awaken his hopes by assuring him that all will be well with him at last; that the heavenly Father, whose child he is, will not permit him to perish; that if his loving discipline does not complete its work in this life, it will be continued in the next until the most wayward of his offspring have been saved.

A young man whom on his death-bed I was earnestly trying to lead to Christ, when near the end of life startled me one day by saying plainly that he knew he "must go to hell" (that was his own language), but hoped he might escape at last, when he had suffered the just punishment of all his sins. I told him earnestly and with deep emotion that, dying with such a lie in his right hand, he had no ground for hoping that he would ever be saved. To my great relief and joy, I found at my next visit that he had not only abandoned the strong and fatal delusion, but that he was rejoicing in the hope of forgiveness and eternal life through Jesus Christ our Lord.

A Universalist friend of mine, the able and popular pastor of a neighboring church, thought I was cruel in the extreme in so dealing with the young man; but the young man himself and his friends were most thankful for the counsel given him, and one of his dying wishes was gratified—that I might support his head when he passed away.

3. The immediate kindred and friends of the

sick and dying have great responsibility for their treatment of their loved ones.

Some utterly ignore the Bible and the Christian religion for themselves and families. Enjoying a thousand blessings of Christianity through life without discerning whence they come, they still, almost without exception, desire for themselves and kindred the rites of Christian burial, but, with strange and dark unbelief, they keep the teachers of religion from the rooms of their sick and dying friends. And yet even they load the caskets of their dead and the tables near them with floral crosses and crowns and harps, as if in solemn mockery of the realities of the gospel which they represent.

One of the last funerals at which I officiated was that of a dock-loafer who fell overboard and was drowned, so far as we know, while plying his unlawful craft and with all his sins upon him. Yet the pure flowers were made to publish him a saint.

Others closely connected with the dying wait till the last moments of life, and then send tearful messengers to some accessible minister to hurry to the sufferer's help, when he ought to have been called weeks before. Quite lately a case of this kind occurred near me. A young man was about to die.

For some time he had felt that his days were numbered, and had asked that a minister might be requested to call. He had seen one of his sisters fade away and die of the same disease. Happily, too, he had heard from her lips words of trust in the Saviour and of the hope of heaven with which she closed her short life and cheered her friends. He longed for a like experience, and repeated his request day after day that some minister might be asked to call. For trivial reasons this simple request was not granted. At last, however, and suddenly, his family saw that he was dying. A sister was despatched in all haste for me. Bathed in tears, she begged me to come quickly. I went immediately with her, but before we reached the house her brother was dead.

There is another class of persons, of whom I speak with great reluctance. They are members of Christian churches. From a perverted love and an erring judgment they keep from the death-room all suggestions of danger to their kindred soon to die, and all the consolations of religion, as if they could in that way exclude death itself.

A letter of a Christian woman known to me from childhood long ago gave me the sad particulars of a case that greatly afflicted her at the time, as the invalid was a very dear personal friend, to whom she would gladly have borne the tidings of salvation by Jesus Christ, but was not permitted to do so, on pain of being excluded from her presence and losing the friendship of the family.

The sufferer was the oldest daughter in a household of great wealth and refinement. Her parents were both members of an evangelical Christian church. They knew, for the physicians had told them, that there was not the least hope of her recovery. They were liberal, kind-hearted and tenderly devoted to their children. Upon this daughter they had bestowed the rarest opportunities of education. All that money could do to minister to the culture of her mind, the gratification of her tastes and her social enjoyment had been freely done. She had traveled widely in other lands, and had "come out," as the phrase goes, with utmost zest in the circles of wealth and fashion in the city where she dwelt. She was known in these circles as singular for the richness and beauty of the laces she wore, the value of her diamonds and other jewels and the general magnificence of her attire.

At length a fatal and very distressing malady fastened itself upon her. A visible and sure decline began, lasting almost a year. Yet all those precious months were spent by her family in the most careful, systematic and successful concealment of the certainty that she must soon die. The physicians, of whom she had several, were charged in no case to whisper her danger or make known the nature of her disease. She was deliberately and often assured that she would soon be able to endure the fatigue of foreign travel. Although daily declining in strength and becoming more and more emaciated, she fondly believed that she would soon be well. When one of her physicians proposed and urged treatment that would leave a stain upon one of her arms for some time, she declined it because she wished soon to appear in society.

This deception on the part of her friends and delusion on her own part continued to the last. When it was known that she might die any day or hour, and certainly could live but a short time, she was promised presents of great value on her recovery, and was allowed to purchase costly jewels to be worn at some future day.

She had Christian friends who yearned over her with inexpressible tenderness. One at least remonstrated with the father, mother and sister. This friend begged the privilege of reading to the sufferer and making known to her her true condition. But she was charged not to interfere with the plan of the family, and, though watching with the sick girl night after night, was never permitted to be with her alone. Even the pastor of the family was allowed to visit her only on condition that he should not make known to her the secret of her near dissolution nor in any way awaken her fears. A very dear friend sent her a beautiful bouquet of flowers, with a note attached referring to their frailty and suggesting hers. The note was detached, and although the girl asked if one did not accompany the flowers, an evasive answer was given, and she was not allowed to see what her friend had sent.

At last the hour of her death came. The family and two physicians were present, watching the flickering flame of life. In a despairing voice the dying one said to one of the physicians, "I believe I am dying." As there was no response, she gasped out the words once more: "Doctor, I believe—I—am—dying." He simply answered, "I understand you." Not even then was a word of helpful truth or earnest prayer uttered in her hearing, and with the sacred name, "O Lord! O Lord!" on her dying lips, she ceased to breathe.

Who of us could bear the responsibility of treating child, sister, friend, parishioner, in this way for months in succession? I think any pastor would be justified in declining to visit a dying person under such restrictions. No wonder that the room where this young woman died was closed to all other occupants, and that parents and friends had great sorrow for many years.

This case does not stand alone. Many reverse the order of the two values, putting the natural life above the eternal, and sinking the latter out of view.

A Christian physician to whom I related the facts given above said that a case similar to it had lately come to his own knowledge. A father whose only daughter was on her death-bed, with but a few days to live, carefully concealed the fact from her. Friends were encouraged to send her presents at his expense, and he said plainly that he would shoot any one who made known to her the certainty that she could live but a short time.

There is one other kind of wrong treatment of the sick and dying that should be noticed with strong disapproval. I mean the multiplying of teachers, the obtrusion upon them of many counselors, and especially if they are of different schools of theology and of strong sectarian habits of mind and heart.

In all critical cases many teachers distract and weary the sufferers. There is danger of having discordant counsels given. And the impression may be made that many guides are needed, as if reliance were placed rather upon the guides than upon Christ, who said, "I am the Way and the Truth and the Life." Even two are not always better than one, unless they have an understanding that they will support each other in uttering the same truths and in trying to arrest and hold attention by such concurrence of testimony, while agreeing together in asking the heavenly Father, in Christ's name, for the salvation of the person or persons whom they earnestly desire to win to Christ.

Unwise friends are in danger of going from one extreme to another—from doing nothing to doing too much. Seized at last with the idea that one whom they love is in peril of his life and is not prepared for the great change, they attach too much importance to the number of teachers, and not enough to a wise choice of one who knows the sick-room well and is faithful and competent in seeking to win souls. Happy the families that are instructed in these great matters, and that are blessed with wise Christian physicians and pastors.

In passing to the second part of our subject,

viz. *The Right Treatment of the Sick and Dying*, I need hardly say that great wisdom and sincere love for the Saviour and the souls of men are always needed. With sanctified common sense one will be very sure quickly to perceive what is best and what should be avoided.

If the sufferers are Christians and are very weak, a few well-chosen words of Scripture and a brief prayer with good cheer from a loving, sympathetic and happy heart may be all-sufficient, and will do good like a medicine.

For an aged disciple of rare intelligence and consecration, belonging to a different denomination from my own, but under my pastoral care, I prepared from day to day, at her own request, brief meditations on suitable texts of Scripture. She was too weak to endure conversation or to meditate profitably by herself, but she could joyfully read a short page of devout thought suggested by different portions of God's word.

I have often been in the rooms of dying saints who could bear only a few whispered words. A pastor or friend refined and sensitive will study and observe all the proprieties of the sick-room, and will find that sometimes silence is better than speech. Sometimes, too, his mission will be best accomplished by merely leaving his name with the family, with the assurance for the sick one that he is remembered in prayer by his pastor. At times, however, it may be inexpedient to leave any message for the sick one who is so low. Then all that the pastor can do will be to call upon the family.

But I am to speak chiefly of the right treatment of the sick and dying who are without the good hope of eternal life in Jesus Christ.

1. A first duty, I think, is to assist in forming a correct public sentiment in regard to the appalling danger of those who fall sick in this sad condition. Let the tidings spread from pulpit to pulpit, from house to house, from suppliant to suppliant. Already there is such a sentiment in reference to persons brought into sudden peril of their bodily lives. A thrill of horror pervades a whole community when it is known that a house in which there are sleepers is on fire or that a child is lost. When I lived in Princeton and was a student in the seminary, a little boy about seven years old, who had been playing in a lumber-yard till a late hour in the afternoon, did not return home and could not be found. He was traced as far on the road to Lawrenceville as a cottage where he had asked for a drink. Near it bars in the fence revealed

a pathway into the fields and clumps of trees. Later it was found that he had passed through these bars. The bells of the seminary and college sounded the alarm. Professors and students and citizens by the hundred came together, were organized into searching parties and went out with lanterns far into the chilly night. Some of us continued the search until the break of day. At last the poor child was found by a bird-dog. He was lying in the deep grass, unconscious, chilled to the bone by the low temperature of the night, and would probably have slept the sleep of death if left to himself. He was borne to his humble home in the strong arms of a man no way related to him as a kinsman. I have never forgotten the thrill of nerve and heart when the tidings rang out through the still air of the morning: "*He is found! He is found, and is living but unconscious.*" Again the bells were rung. Men of all ages and ranks and characters greeted each other with utmost joy. Tears were on many faces in the street and in scores of homes. Every mother felt the gladness of a personal deliverance. And yet that little boy was unknown to most of the men who made long and painful search for him, and not one in a hundred of the men and women who wept for gladness when he was found had any personal knowledge of the child.

There is no deep feeling like this when it is known that one who has no hope in Christ has fallen sick and is in danger of death. Even in such cases the chief anxiety seems to be for the life of the body. The sickness is not taken to heart by many persons as calling for special and persistent effort for the salvation of the soul. We reproach ourselves for want of feeling. We can explain the general indifference only on the mournful theory that in preparation for meeting God safely one need not be greatly concerned about being born again, with faith in the Lord Jesus Christ and holiness at least in its germ.

I think we should do what we can, from the pulpit and the press and by visitation among the people committed to our care, to change this apathy to rational concern. If one falls dangerously sick, who, it is feared, has made no preparation for death, the fact should be known by those of his kinsfolk and acquaintances who believe in the power of prayer. The longest life is well spent only when it is a true preparation for the life beyond. But here one is in great peril, who, it is believed, has yet to take the first step heavenward.

How appalling! But God waits to be gracious. Christ is able to save to the uttermost all who come unto God by him. The Holy Spirit is the Spirit of Truth, the Author and Interpreter of the word which his faithful messengers earnestly make known. He can waken the dead and lead them to Christ; therefore we cherish hope to the last. And this we ought to do all the more fondly if we find ourselves and others as intensely aroused as when the bodily life of child or adult is brought into sudden peril.

2. A duty that cannot be too strongly stated devolves upon those who are nearest the sufferers in family relations.

These have the sick completely in their power. Under a false view of the relation of means to ends—faith and prayer to sickness—some are known to refuse all other agencies for healing. I believe that this folly, to call it by no harsher name, has cost many precious lives. "Faith cure," "Christian science" and "Mind cure" may be classed together. I mention them in this connection only to say with stronger emphasis that those who have very sick persons in their families in all ordinary cases should early call to their help a competent physician, and while carefully obeying his directions should co-operate with him to the utmost of their power. They should be sure not to work against him purposely or by neglect. If the sickness falls upon some poor kinsman or neighbor, let them use their kind offices to secure a physician. It seems almost unnecessary to add that they should be sure of competence and fidelity in the person who is called to guide the sick in the way of life.

3. It is sometimes a perplexing question, Shall minister or physician or any one else inform those who are fatally sick that they cannot recover?

If, beyond all reasonable doubt, the dying are ready for the great change, it is of little consequence whether they are told or not. There may, however, be some matters that they would wish to arrange if they knew that life was about to close—some farewell word they might desire to speak, or some testimony for Christ to give to the living. These are reasons for telling them frankly yet gently that the end is near.

If they are not Christians, and are flattering themselves that they will yet recover while all others believe that they can live but a short time, let them know, as best you can, that life is waning and eternity nearing. I can recall no instance, in a pastorate of more than forty-two years, in which a person unprepared for death, and yet not far from it, could have been wisely deprived of the knowledge of the fact. Such information wisely and tenderly given is of great use in rousing the careless to the necessity of preparing for the change and giving earnest heed to instruction and prayer. I have never known it to destroy or depress the powers of life.

"Conversation does not hurt me," said a young Irishman to Dr. Spencer in one of his last interviews; "and it would be no matter, you know, if it did. I am soon to go. Earth has done with me. The grave lifts up her voice to claim me. I am preparing to say, 'Yes, I come.'" Most of the sick will be found to share in this feeling. If we have dealt openly with them, we cannot well help showing them that our chief concern is for their salvation. They will see that we make everything subordinate to this, and will learn at last, under the teaching of the Holy Spirit, that the gospel they have neglected through life after all is the best gift of God to sinful men, and that all its blessings are as free to them as the service we gladly render or as the air they breathe.

I was once urged by a father whom I well

knew to see his dying son. He had been fatally hurt, and died a few days later. I went with the father at once, but told him by the way that I could take the responsibility of caring for his son only on two conditions: one, that I should have full charge of his instruction; and the other, that I should decide when to tell him that his hurt was fatal. The father gave his consent with tears, fearing that his son could not bear to learn that his end was near. But the father had reason, before the end, to rejoice that he consented.

4. In most cases of fatal sickness the responsibility of being the religious counselor falls, or should fall, upon one person. The duty of the family is partially discharged in making the selection of one believed to be competent for the sacred duty. It may be one of their own number, or some friend of the sufferer, or the pastor of the congregation to which the family belongs. In either case the duties of the one chosen are very serious, and should be well understood.

(1) He ought to be fully convinced that he is called in the providence of God, as well as by the choice of his fellows, to the solemn duty. Otherwise he may have serious misgivings, and at critical moments, when important decisions must be

promptly made, wish that another were in his place. If he is the pastor of the household, he need have little doubt regarding his duty. And yet a devoted Christian minister, who is now venerable for his years and his excellence of character, told me a few days ago that, having been called as a young pastor to visit a dying person in his congregation, he was greatly alarmed, and hardly knew what to say or do, wishing earnestly that he might be relieved from the responsibility of guiding a soul so near to the other world.

(2) It is very important to see the sufferer alone sometimes, if not always. He may wish to make statements about himself that he cannot get his own consent to make in the presence of the family or any one but his religious teacher. When one has lived for years without revealing thoughts and feelings on religious subjects, there is great reluctance to speak of them except confidentially to some one who is accepted as a religious teacher. This is true of persons in health when awakened to ask about the way of life. Every pastor knows that inquirers are apt to seek counsel privately, and not of any in their own families. When, by the grace of God, salvation comes to the anxious soul in health or sickness, the reasons for privacy no

longer exist, but until that time one responsible for telling a dying person what to do to be saved should share in the desire to be without the embarrassment of having others present.

(3) Let a thorough and prayerful study of every case be made, that instruction may be wisely given. Better trust the care of the body to physicians who are careless in their diagnosis and treatment, or to those of different schools of practice, than immortal souls, as yet unsaved, to teachers who make no careful inquiry regarding heredity, temperament, idiosyncrasy, history, character, manner of life, if these are not already known. It is true that "as in water face answereth to face, so the heart of man to man;" yet is it equally true that the dying may differ in many respects from each other, and should be well known by those who are called to give them counsel. Unlike in age and intelligence, they may be still more unlike in regard to the knowledge and treatment of Bible truth, which, so far as we know, is the Holy Spirit's only instrument in saving adult sinners.

(4) In most cases frequent and short visits are better than infrequent and long ones. They are less exhausting to the sick; they are the best proof of sincere love and deep concern; they win confi-

dence, and are most helpful to arouse what may sometimes be a perverted or slumbering conscience; and they serve to fix salutary impressions of vital truths on what may come to be an enfeebled understanding and failing heart. And, besides all this, if there are evidences of the birth from above, there will be need of instruction in the great truths of God's word. Jesus said, "Sanctify them through thy truth: thy word is truth."

(5) One cannot always enter a sick-room when he would gladly do it. A wise and affectionate letter sent through the mail, and then another and another, may open a door otherwise closed, and prove to be the beginning of a blessed ministry. And after the door is open and one has freest entrance, letters may be more helpful than interviews only, for they can be read and often re-read, until the truths they contain are fixed in the mind.

A youth who was known to me to be sinking under pulmonary disease said to his father, in reference to myself, "Ask him to call, but request him to say nothing about religion and not to pray, for that will make me think I am going to die."

I called by invitation, chatted a few moments on commonplace subjects and said good-bye, taking the young man at his word in regard to the subjects of "religion" and "prayer." But I determined to win my way to his sick-room as a messenger of Christ, and, having sent one or two letters to him by mail, I was soon asked to call. I found my letters lying on a stand close beside him, with his Bible there too. The letters had been read more than once, and, finding that he prized them greatly, I continued to write for sixty consecutive days, making frequent visits also. The last letter was written and read on the day of his death. They are now bound, and treasured by the family as the counsel given to one who was very dear to many hearts as he passed from death unto life, and came, before he left us, to the glad confession of Christ, and at the last, as we believe, to the joyful departure to be with Christ.

But whether one speaks or writes to the sick, it should be always remembered that the word of God is the instrument by which the Holy Spirit puts forth his saving power in "convincing and converting sinners and building them up in holiness and comfort through faith unto salvation." Let one think what that word has been and is to himself, and in preparation for his work let him saturate his own soul with it. Then he will speak out of the abundance of his heart. Reading or repeating it, he may wisely give the sense in words easy to be understood. If the meaning is clear, let him rely consciously on the Spirit of Truth to interpret and apply it to the soul. Often it is wise to select passages by book and chapter and verse, and mark them for others to read at the bedside. It is important, too, in the use of Scripture to have regard to the divine order and proportions of truth. The saving work of the Holy Spirit has two principal parts. "When he is come," said Jesus, "he shall reprove the world of sin, and of righteousness, and of judgment." The reasons follow. This is one part. "He shall glorify me, for he shall receive of mine and shall show it unto you." This is the other. It is equally important, for "No man can say that Jesus is the Lord, but by the Holy Ghost." It belongs to him to reveal Christ's divine person, his perfect character, his sacred offices, his redemptive work and his willingness and ability "to save to the uttermost all that come unto God by him." Nor should it be thought enough to point the dying sinner to the divine Saviour as if he were only far away in the heavens. His glorified humanity does not limit his deity. As he dwells in the heart of the believer by faith, it is his privilege to urge the unsaved one to come to the Saviour, to believe that he is present, and, as Dr. James W. Alexander wrote of him, "the most accessible being in the universe." It is our duty and privilege to win souls to Christ, to take them with ourselves to his presence and make intercession for them, giving them to understand that under this ministration of the Spirit they do not need to think of him as coming down out of the heavens to enlighten them in the knowledge of the truth, but rather as passing from the heart of the believer to their hearts.

(6) It is helpful to have knowledge of Christian hymnology for use in the sick-room. If one can sing the sweet truths of the gospel in "psalms and hymns and spiritual songs," so much the better; but care should be taken not to excite mere emotion before the mind is well supplied with Bible truths.

How precious are the hymns beginning with the words "Come, humble sinner, in whose breast;" "I'll go to Jesus though my sins;" "Just as I am, without one plea;" "Jesus, lover of my soul;" "My faith looks up to thee," and many another in common use!

(7) It is a great help to those who are feeling after Christ on a dying bed to be told how others

during their last days have found peace in believing, and have witnessed a good confession before leaving the world. And it gives them great confidence in one who has the responsibility of instructing them to learn from his own lips what the Lord has done for his soul. It is wise, therefore, in some cases to tell the story of one's early faith and, it may be, later conflicts, for the Adversary is often very cruel and aggressive in dealing with those who have but a short time to live.

(8) Having given heed to the important matters already noticed, it remains for one to cast himself in his helplessness upon the God of all grace for direction, support and results. Let him never lose sight of the sovereignty and supremacy of God in saving sinners. It is his prerogative to have mercy upon whom he will have mercy; to send his saving word and renewing Spirit to the heart of the sufferer about to die, or to leave him in the darkness of unbelief and death. Let no one complain of this, but, with sweet and conscious acquiescence in the unknown will of the Lord of life, go on with his humble and beneficent work, giving line upon line, precept upon precept, here a little and there a little of precious truth. Let it be adapted to a case that has been carefully studied;

and it should never be forgotten that in the building of character for eternity, as in the building of the temple-walls in troublous times, the work is not by might nor by power, but by the Spirit of the Lord. One may well rouse himself to intelligent, persistent and hopeful effort by reflecting that the salvation of a soul, always impossible to man, is possible to God in the most adverse circumstances; that "man's extremity is God's opportunity," and that when effected the salvation brings glory to God, produces joy in heaven, gives life eternal to an immortal soul, with large reward here and hereafter to the soul's winner.

For these and other reasons let the minister avail himself of all possible help in his work. The word of God is powerless unless accompanied by the Holy Spirit. He is given in answer to the prayer of faith. In this, as in many other important matters, "two are better than one." Jesus said, "If two of you shall agree on earth as touching anything that they shall ask, it shall be done for them of my Father which is in heaven." The limitations of asking are not hard to find. We act under a divine commission in seeking the salvation of souls; therefore we may assure ourselves that Christ is himself interested in what so deeply concerns us. But we may not dictate while we pray without ceasing. Pray in secret, by the wayside, in the family. We may take the dying and lay them at the feet of Jesus by the faith that makes the transaction very real; remembering that one borne of four was laid at his feet in Palestine, and that when "he saw *their faith*, he said unto him, Man, thy sins are forgiven thee."

Therefore let others come into the secret of the dying sinner's need and peril, and secure their prayers. Let intercessions of faith be offered where Christians meet for prayer, and let the representatives of many homes bear the burden of the imperiled soul away with them, until from many closets and family altars fervent supplications shall be offered to the Hearer of prayer. If they fail to secure the very thing reverently asked for, they cannot fail to bring large benediction to those who offer them. A Christian Church is an organized part of the great kingdom of priests. It is graced with authority and power to make intercession in the name of Christ and to offer the sacrifice of praise and thanksgiving. And every believer may be an Israelite indeed, one of the princes of the earth, having power to prevail with God and men. Meetings for prayer have new interest when they are thus connected with the saving of souls that are ready to perish. The suppliants come to expect triumphs of grace; and as from time to time, in the history of individual churches, tidings come of salvation found even on the bed of death, there will be not only joy in many hearts, but a new consciousness of power for all church work, and a firmer faith that heaven and earth are very near each other and service here a preparation for service there.

It remains now only to notice briefly *some of the uses that may be wisely made of death-bed experiences.*

1. There is great variety in results. Personally, I wish that services for the burial of the dead might be greatly simplified and expenses reduced.

Moreover, if anything is to be said of the departed, it were better reserved, I think, to be spoken at one of the regular services of the house of God. Saving impressions are rarely made on the minds and hearts of unsaved persons who flock to funerals but neglect sanctuaries. True, indeed, "it is better to go to the house of mourning than to go to the house of feasting; for that is the end of all men: and the living will lay it to his heart." But the living who lay it to heart are chiefly those who already have life in Christ.

2. Only in cases that are quite exceptional can a minister wisely speak plainly of the dead who have wasted life and seemingly died in their sins. And then it should be only with the approval of the kindred and for the benefit of the living.

3. If the deceased indulged the hope of salvation only in their last sickness, there is need of careful discrimination in what may be said of them.

In some cases the evidences of repentance and the acceptance of Christ as the Saviour may be most convincing and inspiring to many witnesses. Joy and praise and wonder fill all hearts. There is an opportunity to magnify the grace of God before the living and to instruct and comfort mourners.

4. We ought to keep in mind life-long character, fixed habits, education, employments, associations. We may not make light of the effects of disease and of remedies on the action of the mind and the words of the mouth. Nor should we lose sight of lineage near and remote, ancestral faith and intercessions or the lack of them. Prayers not less than alms are for a memorial before God. A Christian lineage is better than a kingly one. The accumulated intercessions of the pious for many

generations are a power in the kingdom of God's grace. He does not forget them, nor should we. It may be wise to give prominence to this truth in speaking of the dead who, even in their last days, come to the glad recognition of it, and call in faith and repentance upon the God of their fathers and mothers. The streets of villages and cities resound with the joy of those who have found even a child that was lost. Nothing should hinder the thanksgiving of those who have reason to believe that a soul dead in trespasses and sins has been made alive in Christ even on a death-bed.

The Spirit of Truth has preserved for us the written account of the change in the dying robber and his quick entrance into paradise with Jesus himself. The same Spirit may be asked to direct his servants, who desire to know what he will have them do, in helping the living through the experiences of those who have passed away.

5. Records of conversions, the deceased being no longer present with the living, are very different from records of remarkable conversions published to the world by the converts themselves or by others while the subjects of them are still living. One cannot but tremble for professed converts when, shortly after their change, from their own

lips or pens or through the agency of others the story of their conversion is published. It is not every mature Christian who could hear from the pulpit or read in papers secular or religious the story of his new life in Christ and suffer no harm.

But the case is quite different when the converts have left the world. If their experience has been either usual or exceptional, throwing strong light upon God's methods of dealing with souls, as they cannot be hurt by its publication, it may be our duty to give it to the world not only for the comfort of the sorrowing, but for the good of others.

Nor should we pay too much regard to the danger of the irreligious perverting such narratives. Nothing escapes perversion. The goodness of God, the gospel of the grace of God, the loving invitations and commands of God,—all these make their appeal to multitudes in vain. God's ambassadors, sent to publish the tidings and conditions of peace, become a savor of life unto life to some, but of death unto death to others, yet equally a sweet savor of God in them that are saved and in them that perish. Yet is it blessed for them to deliver their message, and leave results with God.

A plain statement of what has been done in behalf of the deceased, of the intense concern felt by many for their salvation, and of the individual and associated efforts to win their souls is a revelation to the world of the great danger of all who are not in Christ, of the nature of Christianity and of what sinners must do to be saved.

The Church itself is edified by accounts of conversions occurring in the last days of life, and the methods God owns in securing them. They help young Christians. They comfort aged saints. They are suggestive to those who have little if any experience in leading souls to Christ. They illustrate the value of the household covenant in many cases. They bear witness to the power of intercessory prayer. They encourage pastors to make record of facts relating to the salvation of souls, which, if not set down at the time, are lost to memory, but, preserved, become precious.

Brethren, my work is done. Imperfect I know it has been. I bring it hither and lay it on your hearts. You hope to live and work for the Master and for souls. Whether here or in other lands, your field will be the world—and the dying world, for which Christ died. Do not despair of any soul while life lasts. Even if reason seems to be dethroned or the soul lost to consciousness, let not even this hinder your confidence in God and in the power of his grace. "I am he that liveth and was dead; and, behold, I am alive for ever more, Amen, and have the keys of hades and of death." These are words of the glorified Christ to the apostle John. No door for their departure out of this life is opened to the dying without his will. Call upon him in faith and submission in their behalf, and though you may not know results with certainty in this life, you will wait calmly, more than satisfied to have him do all his holy pleasure.

I am thankful to the faculty and to you, the students, for the privilege of bringing to this beloved place some of the fruits of pastoral services continued through many years. More than thirty years ago I thought of asking to be allowed to speak to the students then present, but I was timid and did not venture. These later years have added to the strength of my conviction that to despair of the sick and dying and leave them without special solicitude and effort for their salvation is to wrong one's own soul as well as theirs, and to dishonor the gracious Saviour who said to the dying robber, "*To-day shalt thou be with me in paradise.*"

Other Related Titles

A Pastor's Sketches: Volumes 1 & 2

by Ichabod Spencer

Spencer's remarkable ministry was drawing to is close in Brooklyn as John Wells' ministry was beginning, but nonetheless he made a profound impact upon Wells' ministry to the lost. These two volumes by Spencer have sold thousands and thousands of copies and touched hearts the world over. Hear some testimonies:

"Spencer is a master at flushing sinners out of hiding and directing them to Jesus Christ." **-Joel Beeke**

"These Spencer extracts are superb and very sobering." **- Peter Jeffery**

"Spencer patiently and wisely helped bring many to find rest and maturity in Jesus Christ. The fruit of a lifetime's care for God's people was given to the church in these invaluable books." **- Geoff Thomas**

"A Pastor's Sketches is a sobering and challenging reminder that the Holy Spirit is the true agent of conversion. This book is urgently needed today." **- Jerry Bridges**

"Spencer's 'Sketches' are a veritable treasury of pastoral wisdom. They will amply repay careful reading by pastors and serious Christians in our day." **- Maurice Roberts**

"Sketches is a splendid and unique volume. I would make it compulsory reading for seminarians in a pastoral theology course." **- Gordon Keddie**

"These sketches show a doctrinal depth and experiential savvy perfectly meshed in one who had the cure of souls as his passion." **- Tom Nettles**

Retail Price is $14.99 each

www.ingramcontent.com/pod-product-compliance
Lightning Source LLC
LaVergne TN
LVHW091006080826
845145LV00003B/1143